CUSTOMER SERVICE EXCELLENCE FOR POLICE

101 Tips on Policing in Cross-Cultural Communities

Amanda Coleman-Mason, Ph.D.
& June Davidson, Ph.D.

© 2017 by Amanda Coleman-Mason

All rights reserved. No part of this book maybe reproduced in any form or by any means without prior permission from the author except for brief quotations embodied in critical essay, article or review. These articles and/ or reviews must state the correct title and contributing authors of this book by name.

Printed in the United States of America

ISBNs: 978-0-9984248-4-2 (print)
        978-0-9984248-5-9 (ebook)

Cover by: Dadeziner-Fiverr Graphics Design

Formatting by: Patti Frazee at pattifrazee.com

Published by:

Black House Publishings
7400 Metro Blvd. Suite 224
Edina, MN 55439
www.blackhousepublishings.com

Testimonials

I worked with Dr. Amanda Coleman-Mason, President of Adissa Justice Leadership Coaching, in her group coaching sessions. I appreciate her insight about active listening since this is such an important skill as I work with clients on the phone and face to face. I learned new ways of listening that allow my clients and me to keep our lines of communication open and clear. And I learned to enhance communication skills that keep me constantly and continuously in tune with my client. I highly recommend Dr. Coleman-Mason for her skillful direction.

— Brenda Gayle Bryant
The Gayle Group
Author, *FSL-Finance as a Second Language*

I needed an Accountability Coach as I hit a wall during the writing of my newest book 101 Tips for Restaurant Success. I reached out to Amanda Coleman-Mason and with Amanda's help and guidance I was able to overcome my writer's block and finish my latest book. Amanda is caring and insightful and through her expert coaching technique Amanda, I found my way. I would reach out to Dr. Amanda Coleman-Mason anytime I find myself struggling. Thank you, Amanda!

— John E Anderson, Restaurant Consultant,
Author, *101 Tips for Restaurant Success*
Coaching Firm International, Certified Business Coach

I am so very impressed with this book as it is not just a great book of ideas and strategies, it is also a spectacular one. It can only be described as a labor of love and a uniquely researched collection of soft skills and tips for community policing while interacting with diverse communities. I find this book to be a must read book that highlights the importance of personal awareness and in promoting and strengthening communication in all areas of relationship building, while providing customer service excellence and justice leadership. This book is the key to making positive inroads in interpersonal relationships!

— Resmaa Menakem, LCSW
CEO Justice Leadership Solutions
Life, Leadership, & Legacy:
101 Tips for Emerging Justice Leaders

With the indifference and cynical views on law enforcement in today's society, this book offers an unapologetic and refreshing set of ideas for law enforcement officers who want to challenge themselves in practicing customer service excellence in their community. Customer Service Excellence for Police provides a multitude of tangible and practical techniques and tips for closing the ever-widening gap between the public and law enforcement while inspiring professional growth. It offers community police officers with the appropriate tools for building community relationships without sacrificing preventive crime techniques while also, shattering old paradigms in law enforcement and community-police relations.

— Kenneth Watson
Detective, Dallas Police Dept.

Why You Need This Book

This guide of 101 beneficial soft skills tips includes strategically placed Challenges to assist you in understanding the provided tips. Do not pass by the Challenges. Rather, engage yourself and allow yourself to delve into the different patterns of thinking and reflections about your work, and your investment in what you do. To get the most out of each Challenge... Stop and engage before you move forward!

Further, you will see that some ethnic terminology (Dr. Maulana Karenga, 1966) has been introduced in this book to emphasize skills and techniques. The intent of the association of these terms is to provide ancestral wisdom and profound thought in the development of each tip.

Table of Contents

Forward xi

Value in Customer Service Excellence xv

Introduction xvii

Chapter 1
Mastery of Self-Awareness 1

Chapter 2
Mastery of Self-Development 13

Chapter 3
Mastery of Attitude Possession 31

Chapter 4
Mastery of Goal Setting 55

Chapter 5
Mastery of Community and
Customer Service Excellence Skills 63

Chapter 6
Mastery of Communication
and Effective Listening 81

Summary 97

Afterword 99

Endnotes 101

Notes 103

Acknowledgments 133

About Adissa Justice Leadership Coaching 135

About the Authors 139

Forward

In this book, *Customer Service Excellence for Police: 101 Tips for Policing in Cross-Cultural Communities*, Dr. Amanda Coleman-Mason has pulled together an eclectic, interesting, and inspiring collection of life lessons, words to live by, sage advice, and pearls of wisdom. While the primary focus of this work is to help strengthen the interpersonal skills of today's professional law enforcement officers in diverse communities, the *101 Tips* presented here, clearly has value to a much wider audience, as well.

Each of the book's six chapters deals with the subconscious mindset and the masteries of self-awareness, self-development, attitude positioning, goal strategies, and effective listening strategies. These chapters address complex community challenges and they also, offer distinctly different approaches to the development of interpersonal and relationship building skills while serving customers. The tips presented here were selected from a wide spectrum of philosophers, authors, thinkers, political and spiritual leaders, entrepreneurs, and more. The tips matched

Dr. Coleman-Mason's coaching strategies, training strategies, and insights into the underpinnings of *Customer Service Excellence*. The cleverly demonstrated writings in the collection of *101 Tips* is a must read for the practitioners of customer service excellence and justice leadership.

— Cliff Jaynes, Chief of Police
University of North Texas, Dallas

Justice is rather the activity of truth than a virtue in itself. Truth tells us what is due to others, and justice renders that due.

—Horace Walpole

CUSTOMER SERVICE EXCELLENCE FOR POLICE

**101 Tips on Policing
in Cross-Cultural Communities**

FORWARD BY CLIFF JAYNES

Amanda Coleman-Mason, Ph.D.
& June Davidson, Ph.D.

Value in Customer Service Excellence

Merely satisfying customers will not be enough. Instead, the customer must experience exceptional service. Customer service excellence is more than what an organization says or does. It means to under promise the services while exceeding the customer's expectations and creating the aura of being pleasantly surprised.

— Rick Tate, Author
One Minute Manager

Steps in Providing Customer Service Excellence:
- Know the Customer and Their Needs
- Build Interpersonal Relationships
- Listen to Customer's Needs
- Practice Continuous and Persistent Learning
- Never Become Complacent about Performance

Introduction

Kirst-Ashman (2014) describes a community as "a number of people who exist with a common interest that distinguishes them from others." Yet, individuals can also exist in a community even though cultural dynamics, ethnicity, and language barriers, etc., prevail. The concern is in finding that proverbial 'sweet spot' that allows interpersonal relationships within that community to flourish. In this 21st century, global challenges in the development and building of effective relationships between cross-cultural communities and community policing agents exist. Common are the struggles of communication, tolerance, and cultural acceptance. The knowledge of those who actively serve in community policing and their ability to provide efficient service (customer service excellence) and justice leadership relies on effective police training, tactics, experience, and skills.

In this 21st century, community policing is found to be directly related to providing and executing *Justice Leadership* in the face of societal and cultural denials, particularly in deeply divided societies and where minority (not the dominant culture) perceptions of police are controversial. As you engage with multi-cultural communities, you can exalt courage, push for change and establish communal relationships, while attempting to deliver customer service excellence. Your actions, however, should be founded on justness, communal resilience, equitability, and service to others (Menakem, 2017). If your goal as a community policing agent is to provide excellence in customer service, it goes without saying that you should attempt to understand the historical and generational concerns that may undermine the impartial or equitable justice that community members deserve. Furthermore, your charge should include understanding the cultural differences such as language, religion, customs, and social and family controls that could impair the building of productive interpersonal relationships.

This discussion of *Justice Leadership* is not complete without mentioning the sometimes abhorrent rhetoric and actions related to the scapegoating of immigrants and minority communities. Blaming or finding reasons to place the social ills of a nation or society upon the shoulders of newcomers or immigrants in America, as well as other countries who have experienced waves of immigration, is not a recent phenomenon. In fact, the act of scapegoating has taken new wings and flies in the face of *Justice Leadership* in the year of 2018. Scapegoating undermines the ability to be productive in building relationships between the community and its policing forces. What better way to connect the concepts of equitable justice and communal resilience than through sound and evidence-based practices? Both may be achieved through consistent and timely *"residency training"* (ongoing awareness). Implementation of ongoing awareness takes place in the form of face to face engagement and it should also include written enforcement such as this book of tips, *Customer Service Excellence for Police: 101 Tips on Policing in Cross-Cultural Communities.*

History of Community Policing

Community policing originated in 1829 in the UK which was developed by Sir Robert Peel. Known as the father of community policing, Peel's characterization was that "community policing was a Philosophy, not a program or a cycle of programs." He determined that the foundation of community policing consisted of five basic principles:

1. Prevent crime and enhance social order through fair and just practices;

2. Secure and maintain public respect;

3. Seek to preserve public favor, but not by pandering to public opinion;

4. Build and maintain relationships with community customers; and

5. Ensure that the outcome of community policing is efficient in the absence of crime and disorder (Larabee, A. K., 2007).

Today's model of community policing, as society knows it, came into focus after the implementation of the Violent Crime Control and Enforcement Act of 1994. This new model reshaped traditional policing from its tendency to be reactive with a concentration on crime control, to preventive or proactive policing strategies that focus on working creatively on solving problems and building communal ties. Furthermore, community policing embraces the transition from a warrior mentality to a guardian mentality and from a sole enforcement mindset to a service mindset. For these proactive and preventive strategies to be successful, they must be accepted and practiced by everyone in the policing department (Paterson, J., n.d.).

Chapter 1

Mastery of Self-Awareness

Every human being has four endowments, self-awareness, conscience, independent will, and creative imagination. These give us the ultimate human freedom...the power to choose, to respond to change.

—Stephen R. Covey, Author
7 Habits of Highly Successfully People

Tip 1: Open Your Mind

You have a choice in life to accept your position or change it.

* * * * *

If you choose to move along in your career of community police work hoping that something or others will change for the better, then you will not get very far. If you want to be a community police agent who provides customer service excellence and unity in the community you serve, then open your mind and seek information to advance change and positioning in your life.

> *The greatest discovery of my generation is that human beings can alter their lives by altering their attitude of mind.*
>
> —William James
> Psychologist, Philosopher

Tip 2: Be Consistent: Take the Long Road in Your Work

There are no shortcuts to anywhere worth going. Taking shortcuts leads to imperfection and inadequacies. Always strive for the best, even if it requires a little more time and effort as it may lead to long-term results. An old cliché states "Anything worth doing is worth doing well." This cliché should be your motto in community policing.

* * * * *

When you want to succeed, taking short-cuts is not an option. Community police who provide or desire to provide customer service excellence to cross-cultural communities and divided societies must consist of a trained workforce with a leadership mindset. That mindset must take on a consistent commitment in refining human interaction and interpersonal relationships. For example, a consistent commitment can include an in-depth bi-annual 6-8 hour training program that seeks to build valuable interpersonal relationships, communication, and customer service etiquette if it's viewed as a long-term investment. It is not beneficial, however, to participate in short-term annual 2-hour orientations or trainings with the intent to superficially satisfy a long-term training process. A steadfast mindset of consistency and a willingness to commit in the long run will likely lead to favorable long-term outcomes.

> *Success is the sum of small efforts,*
> *repeated day in and day out.*
>
> —Robert Collier, Author
> *Riches Within Your Reach*

Tip 3: Kujichagulia: Take Responsibility

Taking responsibility (*Kujichagulia*[1]) is your self-determined intentional act to do the correct thing. Before we can correct a mistake, we must first own it, and do it quickly! If it was your choice and your wrong decision, then assume accountability and be ready to agree on the consequences.

* * * * *

Have you set a firm milestone in your career in which you intend to complete your educational goals that can be of benefit to you in your community policing? If so, you are probably aware that you need to accomplish these educational goals so that you can effectively interact in a leadership capacity with your customers in the community.

If you allowed distractions to conflate your goals and intentions, time will not be on your side, and you'll miss your educational opportunity. And so, you may witness stifling problems related to community disenchantment and a lack of trust in the services that you and your fellow officers provide. Your previous poor judgment could be costly, as you're the only one to be held responsible for the missed opportunity in showing some grounded leadership skills in developing interpersonal relationships and goodwill in the community.

> *More is required of public officials than slogans, handshakes, and press releases. We must hold ourselves strictly accountable, and we must provide the people with a vision of the future.*
>
> —Barbara Jordan,
> Texas Congresswoman, Civil Rights Leader

Tip 4: Nia: Embrace the Art of Giving

People who are sincere about sharing and giving, do so unselfishly and out of the goodness of their hearts with a designed *purpose*.

* * * * *

Knowing how to "give" excellent customer service in community policing is the key to great community relations, as community policing is more than a physical act. It pertains to a sharing and giving partnership, coupled with a philosophy of personalized full-service policing. In this relationship, community policing agents interact and work with *purpose* and with a goal of identifying and solving problems with earnest sincerity. If you practice this art of giving, the community will return it in the same manner.

> *Relationships work best when you think of relationships as a vehicle of giving and contributing, and as a secular spiritual practice of keeping your interests present but not predominant in your choice processes.*
>
> —Paul Richards
> Athlete

Tip 5: Be Authentic

Being authentic means staying true to who you are; what you do and how you serve.

* * * * *

What we can learn from the deeply divided society of Ferguson, MO, is that poor ethical leadership and social policies; the lack of personal integrity and community accountability; unaddressed social factors; and the lack of authenticity can destroy the brand of effective community policing, unity (Umoja), and justice leadership in a community. Most of these elements often become the contributors toward poor communication, disrespect, community relations and thereby, poor customer service.

Authenticity:

- Reflects your identity, image and creates influence in the community.
- Enables people to develop confidence in your interactive community skills.
- Draws people in the community towards you.
- Reveals you as a reliable and trustworthy community servant. Encourages engagement and citizen advocacy.

> *Someone who takes the time to understand their relationship with source, who actively seeks alignment with their broader perspective, who deliberately seeks and finds alignment with who-they-really-are, is more charismatic, more attractive, more effective and more powerful than a group of millions who have not achieved this alignment.*
>
> —Abraham Hicks, Author,
> *Law of Attraction*

Tip 6: Transform Your Image

Make a list of things that make you happy. Make a list of things you do every day. Compare the list. Adjust accordingly.

* * * * *

To succeed at community policing and providing customer service excellence, you will likely first determine that you have the potential or tools to reach your professed goals. For instance, if you want to become the commander of your community unit, but you have no formal management training in policing, then you may feel that success in this area is not likely to happen. However, being a past leader in your ROTC unit in high school or having a military leadership background may be a bonus. When coupled with your completed police training program, this could be just the path for you to take to move forward as a unit leader. By transforming your past leadership performance and experiences, you have the potential to achieve your desired success.

> *Transformation is not five minutes from now; it's a present activity. In this moment you can make a different choice, and it's these small choices and successes that build up over time to help cultivate a healthy self-image and self-esteem.*
> —Jillian Michaels
> Fitness Instructor

Tip 7: Conquer Your Fear of Failure

If we are to be successful in our work, then we ought to have an understanding about why we may let fear hold us back. But, in most instances, it's not "failing" itself that strikes fear onto us. More often than not, it is the unobvious outcomes following the failure that prompts our fear and retreat.

* * * * *

For example, losing your leadership position as Traffic Safety Liaison can be upsetting on its merit. For you, your loss of position may pose more embarrassment to you than the actual loss itself, as it undermines your confidence and passion concerning the work you perform in the community. You may even question whether you should seek another position related to your work as you feel stuck in your loss. However, remaining stuck is not an option.

Move Past Fear by:
- Changing your perceptions of the failure.
- Finding a Coach, Mentor or listening partner.
- Re-examining and realigning your goals.
- Breaking down your goals into doable chunks.
- Believing in yourself and your desires.

> *Fear of failure must never be seen as a reason not to try something.*
> —Frederick Smith
> CEO of FedEx

Tip 8: Practice Self-Confidence & Belief in Yourself

When was the last time you found yourself in an emotional slump? At that time, did you lose sight of yourself and your abilities? Did you lose your balance in your work? You are more than you believe you are. Prove it by getting other "people's opinions out of your head" and be instrumental in defining yourself. Remember, it is their opinion and not yours.

* * * * *

As you work towards the goal of being a balanced and knowledgeable community servant who is engaged in performing community customer service excellence, it is essential to your success that you not only need to believe in the service that you provide, but you also need to believe in yourself. How will you influence community and interpersonal relationships if you lack self-confidence and self-efficacy? Believing in yourself relates to your level of self-confidence and the belief in your capability to move forward in building upon a community relationship that you can influence in fostering trust, respect, and credibility. You must master the skills of self-belief and self-confidence.

> *Low self-confidence isn't a life sentence. Self-confidence can be learned, practiced, and mastered—just like any other skill. Once you master it, everything in your life will change for the better.*
>
> —Barrie Davenport, Author
> *Peace of Mindfulness*

Tip 9: Take Time for Reflection

When we reflect, we learn from our mistakes. If we do not reflect, the chances are high that we will repeat those mistakes. We can benefit from our mistakes through meditation. Meditation allows us to determine the errors of our ways, correct them, and prevent them in the future.

* * * * *

As you make your way toward success, you'll need to focus on the big picture as small and large obstacles can prevail. Maintain confidence and pick your battles wisely. Allow time for yourself to think without interruption and disconnect. Quietly and solemnly reflect on what you have accomplished to ensure that you are moving in your desired direction. Instead of being entrenched in an endless battle over an issue, step back and reflect.

> *You have to choose your path. You have to decide what you wish to do. You are the only person that can determine your destiny.*
> —Lailah Gifty Akita, Author
> *Think Great: Be Great!*

Tip 10: Review Your Perspectives and Judgment

Your perspective and intuitive judgment require periodic consideration and scrutiny concerning your career and your successes in your work performance.

* * * * *

Your work perspective is the way that you look at and the way you see yourself in community policing. Is it right for you? Assumptions of our past experiences can come together to form new thought perspectives and intuitive judgment. For example, your views on the work and community services you perform should be periodically reexamined. As your awareness levels rise and you acknowledge and understand your job in community policing, you may embrace a different perspective of your career. You won't know this unless you "step back" and review your professional work in serving the community and its customers.

Review the challenge concerning *"what you see."* Now, step back and review this challenge again. A different view can provide a different way that this challenge looks to you, right?

The Challenge:

by Michael Michalko

❝ *When you change the way you look at things, the things you look at change.*

—Wayne Dyer, Author
The Power of Intention

Tip 11: Become an Expert—Application and Practice Mean Everything

You need to feel confident and competent. In your area of expertise, take on those responsibilities that you know you excel in, and don't forget to ask for help when you find yourself struggling.

* * * * *

You should practice doing things rather than simply learning about them and doing nothing. Some behavioral scientist report that in the routine of training and performance the *"ten-year rule"* or *"10,000-hour rule,"* is needed to achieve an expert level of performance in any given field of work. Accordingly, some scientists recommend the quality of time over quantity.

The adage: *"Practice makes perfect"* is not enough. Your belief in yourself and your ability to seek and apply the information and skills that you gain, while interacting with the community you serve are all valuable tools. When used succinctly, they will take you closer to becoming an expert in your field of community policing.

> *It had long since come to my attention that people of accomplishment rarely sat back and let things happen to them. They went out and "happened to things."*
> —Leonardo Da Vinci, Artist

Tip 12: Understand Your Implicit Biases

As you perform your duties and responsibilities in community policing, you will likely come face to face with biases. Biases can be positive or negative aspects of human nature and biases can be implicit, as well. Implicit bias refers to attitudes or stereotypes that may have an impact on your ability to understand, perform certain actions, and make unconscious decisions.

* * * * *

The implicit bias can be activated involuntarily and without the individual's awareness and unfavorable control. As these biases reside deep in the subconscious mind, they are different from known biases. A common characteristic of implicit biases is that it may cause you to "choose to conceal" your behavior for social and political correctness.

* * * * *

It's important that you meet the object of your bias head on with an open mind. The most efficient and yet the hardest way to do this is to meet it face to face. Look for the "*humanity*" in the object of your prejudice. Remembering that everyone is human and has feelings, thoughts, wishes, and dreams is the key to your success in this area. While working in diverse and cross-cultural communities, it is important that you know that everyone identifies with their culture. Recognize that their culture is isolated from yours and has developed historical differences.

A positive interpersonal relationship between you as a community policing agent and the community you serve is connected by your real understanding and acceptance of the dynamics of implicit bias. Implicit bias training can help community policing agents have a better encounter with the community being served.

> *The eye sees only what the mind is prepared to comprehend.*
>
> —Robertson Davies
> Tempest-Tost

Chapter 2

Mastery of Self-Development

*Breaking old habits and forming new ones
always takes time, but it is worth it in the end.*
—Joyce Meyer, Christian Minister,
Author, *Power Thoughts*

Tip 13: Embrace Your Discomfort to Find New Opportunities

Embrace discomfort! Why would you want to embrace discomfort? Most people would have this type of response and reaction to such a statement. The reality is that people do not naturally embrace fear, as the unknown element(s) of situations and concerns make people uncomfortable.

* * * * *

A portion of our brain that tells us to run when we face unknown and uncomfortable situations. In the review of a six-year veteran female liaison police officer in South Texas, who was due to be transferred to another station in a larger community, reluctance was born out of fear. She would be leaving an area that served a community that was once untrusting and wary of the community police agents. But over time a level of trust was built within the community as interpersonal relationships grew as a result of open dialogue and effective communication.

Rather than allow her fears to control her thoughts, the officer took control over those negative and fearful thoughts and embraced her move to the new station. She reached out and met her new co-workers. In doing so, she gained an understanding of the community prior to her move. When the time came to make the transition, it went smoothly. She found that she had some experiential solutions and ideas that were welcomed by the new community. Studies consistently show that the most successful people in their field of expertise embrace discomfort and they often thrive on it.

> *Where there is no challenge,
> there is no opportunity for change or success.*
> — Anonymous

Tip 14: Don't Buy Into Shortcuts and Temporary Solutions

Considering the average person's lifespan is approximately 75 years and you will likely spend 1/3 of it sleeping, life may seem too short! Should you consider or hope to take the hard way to every little problem that you may encounter, or take a shortcut to success?

* * * * *

The reality is that shortcuts are often based on ignorance and a lack of understanding, as they can sometimes result in more work, rather than less work. So, when the common focus becomes *"finding temporary solutions or shortcuts"* instead of finding ways to be successful, the wrong habits can develop and undermine your actual goals and purpose. These practices can lead you from one shortcut to another – without learning anything new or even realizing that you may be spending more time and energy on temporary solutions.

> *When you live for a strong purpose, then hard work isn't an option. It's a necessity.*
> —Steve Pavlina, Author
> *Personal Development for Smart People*

Tip 15: Nia: Purposefully Manifest Your Dreams

To succeed, you need to be purposeful or focused on your *"why,"* or the reasons you do *"what"* you do and *"how"* you do them.

* * * * *

Most people have dreams, and everyone has goals at some point. Bringing your goals into reality requires that you be consistent and also embrace *"responsible purpose"* (Nia^2). Consistency is about being responsible and restoring your purpose through focus. Pareto's 80/20 observation addresses the principle that 80% of your achievements are the outcome of 20% of your labor. Translation? Are you utilizing and focusing your purpose effectively to achieve what you want out of life? Being in a purposeful mindset will allow you to maximize your efforts and achieve the outcomes you seek.

If you want to become a leader, say, a Police Chief, you need to maximize your efforts in all areas of your life. Look at those who've preceded you and take the time to focus your purpose on "*why*," which will lead you to the "*what*" and "*how*" of your goal. Anything less than this outline of purposeful thinking is wishful thinking.

> *Stay focused, go after your dreams and keep moving toward your goals.*
> —LL Cool J, Musician-Actor

Tip 16: Kuumba: Use Creativity in the Law of Attraction

Embrace the Law of Attraction to manifest your dreams by being creative. The goal is to create opportunities and focus on the "*outcomes*" you desire. The Law of Attraction requires that you adjust your conscious thoughts, beliefs, and behavior.

* * * * *

You'll need to undo the unproductive negative habits and patterns that you've stored in your unconscious mind. Show creativity (*Kuumba*[3]) by replacing negative elements with inspiring engaging actions. Rewire your brain to attract likeness, which means that you must refrain from storing the layers of limiting beliefs, fears, and negative experiences. You must begin to consciously and habitually think positive creative thoughts; not only about yourself but also about the community you serve. Remembering that "*your thoughts attract similar situations and circumstances*" is the key to manifesting your dreams.

> *The biggest adventure you can take is to live the life of your dreams.*
> —Oprah Winfrey, Entrepreneur

Tip 17: Appreciate Your Contributions

Your contributions to your workplace reveal your actual development as a servant leader. Step back into a quiet place and acknowledge your worth.

* * * * *

Your efforts, attitudes, ideas, participation, and the way that you tackle your duties, tasks, and responsibilities all channel your professionalism. While you look for the needs of those you serve, be mindful as to how you communicate with your community partners and how you contribute to solving the problems, issues, and concerns as a servant leader. These aspects are precious to you in community policing. Quietly acknowledge your value and worth in your servant leadership development.

> *It is one of the most beautiful compensations of life that no man can sincerely try to help another without helping himself. Serve and you shall be served.*
> —Ralph Waldo Emerson, Essayist Transcendental Movement Leader

Tip 18: Be Flexible and Adaptable to Differences

Flexibility, the ability to change or compromise, is today's new norm. Embracing flexibility and being nimble-minded, particularly, when interacting with customers in community policing, reveals that you value community diversity and that you can successfully manage those differences.

* * * * *

In today's awareness of the impact of diversity in community policing, we recognize its values of diversity, flexibility, and adaptation as the new norm. Differing cultures, religions, and community needs mean that today's community servants must accommodate diversity when it comes to relationship building, listening, and communicating with others.

> " *The measure of a person's strength is not their muscular power or strength, but it is their flexibility and adaptability.*
> —Debasish Mridha, Physician

Tip 19: Improve Your Efficiency

When you improve your efficiency by developing your potential to its fullest, you also increase your output in "what you get done."

* * * * *

You should implement effective strategies to increase your productivity using the "*work smarter rule.*" This rule means that you must employ time restraints, be proactive rather than reactive, eliminate procrastination, maintain constant focus and make certain that those you work with honor and respect your efficiency strategies.

> *When you waste a moment, you have killed it in a sense, squandering an invaluable opportunity. But when you use the moment correctly, filling it with purpose and productivity, it lives on forever.*
> -Rabbi Menachem Mendel Schneerson
> Religious Leader

Tip 20: Know What You Don't Know and Seek Input

Law enforcement personnel who have gotten to the level of Sergeant, Lieutenant, Captain, or higher, whether at a large or small police department, are there because they knew they didn't have all the answers and they were receptive to continuous learning and improvement. They knew what they didn't know.

* * * * *

Challenge yourself and get input from others. Accomplished police commanders, who are at the top of their game, are experts at taking criticism and feedback from those they admire and respect. Successful people take on jobs that are likely to challenge them. And in the face of challenge *"they know what they don't know."* Their attitude of continuous learning and feedback from their peers attributes greatly to their successful outcomes.

> *He that knows not, and knows that he knows not is a pupil. Teach him. He that knows and knows that he knows is a teacher. Follow him.*
> —Arab Proverbs

Tip 21: You Don't Have to Settle

Settling is about not embracing what is best for you and accepting what you don't want. When you settle you take less than you deserve. Settling can become a habit and a way of life, but it doesn't have to be. According to Bo Bennett (2004), every day, people settle for less than they deserve. *They settle, sometimes out of fear, which can often create feelings of being stuck and preventing them from embracing what they want.*

* * * * *

Some people settle for unsatisfying jobs, boring lives, and old relationships. People establish themselves in part because they don't realize they can have better, or even that they deserve better. An excellent example of this concerns a community police agent, Officer Davis, who worked in a suburban Cleveland community. He had given lots of thought to organizing a community Children's Special Olympics team for several years. Davis repeatedly said that he'd pursue his dream someday. Davis' statement meant that: "when some unknown thing happened, then he would do that thing that he wanted to do." So, Officer Davis was not getting what he wanted; rather he was settling. *Never settle for anything less than you believe you deserve.*

> " *The minute you settle for less than you deserve, you get even less than you settled for.*
> —Maureen Dowd, Journalist

Tip 22: Umoja: Be a Good Leader — A Good Servant

The servant-leader is a servant first. It begins with the natural feeling that you want to serve first. As a servant-leader, a conscious choice brings you to aspire to lead.

* * * * *

You are a person who is sharply different from someone who is a leader first because you have a need to diminish your power drive or to acquire material possessions. As a servant-leader, you focus primarily, on the growth and well-being of people and the community to which you serve. *The servant-leader believes in unity (Umoja[4]), shares power, and puts the needs of others first and helps people develop and perform as highly as possible.*

> *Good leaders must first become good servants.*
> —Robert Greenleaf,
> Founder of Greenleaf Center
> for Servant Leadership

Tip 23: Seek Out, Enroll, and Welcome Training

Treat every day as a learning experience. The day you know everything about community policing, you should turn in your shield. *The idea is to keep learning, and never, ever quit learning. Seek out, enroll, and welcome training as a new experience.*

* * * * *

To keep pace with the ever-changing migration and movement of people, along with fast developing community needs, the knowledge and skills of community police agents needs to be continuously upgraded. Balancing learning and individual self-learning to keep pace is a must. An example of this strategy is executed with precision in most progressively thriving countries in which police organizations must interact with local and cross-cultural communities in providing effective solutions for its customers. Balanced learning can also be achieved through a type of "*residency training.*" Just as medical professionals engage in a committed residency to apply learning in a practical experience, junior community policing agents can incorporate their technical skills with their self-development as they progress in their cross-cultural and communal relationships.

> "Those people who develop the ability to continuously acquire new and better forms of knowledge that they can apply to their work and their lives will be the movers and shakers in our society for the indefinite future.
>
> —Brian Tracy, Author
> *Personal Success: The Brian Tracy Success Library*

Tip 24: Don't Run from Change

Changing patterns is difficult for some, particularly if the objective is related to community behavioral changes. In cross-cultural communities where it is imperative that understanding and adaptation be embraced, the change process can bring about confliction and fear, due to the familiarity you've embraced.

* * * * *

Stand firm, focus, and give behavioral change a chance to succeed in the community you serve. You may even feel as though you are stuck as some in the community may still offer resistance to agreed-upon changes and efforts. As a community policing agent, take the time to adjust your thoughts and your behaviors as well. The easiest thing to do is to keep walking forward, even if it takes substantial time, and trial and effort, to undue the behavior that has become familiar and comfortable to you.

> *When we are no longer able to change a situation,*
> *we are still challenged to change ourselves.*
> —Victor E. Frankl
> Austrian Neurologist

Tip 25: Balance the Concepts of "Ordinary and Comfortable" in Your Life

Author, F. M. Alexander, stated that: "*Unfortunately, we have been taught that all the everyday acts of life should be automatic and unconscious if we desire comfort.*" For this reason, people have become comfortable in their ordinary day-to-day interactions and do not see the need to expand or change their circumstances.

* * * * *

"*There is an absolute temperature (familiarity) at which we feel the most comfortable.*" There is a way of life in which we feel at ease because it is the ordinary. There may even be a group of people with whom we feel most comfortable. But when it seems that we are around the wrong people because of differences or in a bad situation, because the *event seems unfamiliar*, we can feel very uncomfortable and out of place. When you are serving customers in community policing, allowing your temperature to not rise by expanding your comfort zone can interfere with interpersonal relationship building, trust, and communication. Raising your temperature and moving beyond your comfort zone can be critically important when serving customers in cross-cultural communities.

> *Coming out of your zone is tough in the beginning, chaotic in the middle, and awesome in the end. Because in the end, it shows you a whole new world. Make an attempt.*
>
> Manoj Arora, Author
> *From the Rat Race to Financial Freedom*

Tip 26: Don't Rest on Success

When things are going well with your interpersonal and relationship-building processes in the cross-cultural community you serve, you must not rest on the assumption that you are on top of everything. You will need to maintain focus and vigilance as you grow in understanding the community you serve.

* * * * *

As time moves forward there will always be existing blind spots. Your ability to consistently reach for new ideas, partnerships, and problem-solving ideas are important to your diverse community. In community policing, exploiting the successes of other communities and possibly other countries as they tackle their concerns related to awareness, understanding, relationship building, and communication can be an effective strategy. The important factor here is to maintain an "*active balance of new ideas*" and to acknowledge the subtle but recognizable changes in the community as they occur.

> *It is fine to celebrate success. But its best to continue to stay balanced and focused on the life-cycle called change.*
>
> —Danielle Kanden
> American Figure Skater

Tip 27: Take Initiative – Apply What You Learn

"Doing" is a much more powerful tool than simply reading or watching. The latest research on brain activity suggests that repetitive practice strengthens neural connections, which are the basis for memory.

* * * * *

In your community policing work, be aware that you must do more than remembering those *"knowledge items."* You must practice using those items in situations that are similar or real as they relate to your work. Sometimes the application can only be practiced in a simulated environment, which can be sufficient, as well.

An excellent example of this practice was the moment when pilot Chesley B. Sullenberger III, safely ditched an American commercial jet into the Hudson River in New York, thereby saving the lives of 155 people on board the plane. It was Sullenberger's simulation training that saved the day. Practice and repetition with a flight simulator and walk-throughs of cabin procedures prepared everyone for the safety applications that saved the lives of everyone on board the airplane. Practice, practice, practice is the key to being prepared for the unpredictable changes in cross-cultural communities and interpersonal relationship building.

> *Wisdom without application is worthless.*
> — Anonymous

Tip 28: Keep A Journal – It's Healthy

Influential people in history have kept detailed journals of their lives and their work. *Journals can serve two purposes:*

a permanent record for the future, and they provide a soothing, cathartic release for the people who write them.

* * * * *

You can receive great benefits immediately, even if you don't think you need to keep a journal. Writing can do wonders for your health, particularly in high-stress public jobs like community policing. A University of Iowa study showed that journaling about stressful events helped participants deal with the events they experienced. Besides being an emotional release, writing a journal can be a great boost for your self-esteem.

> *What a comfort is this journal. I tell myself to myself, and through the burden of my book, I feel relieved.*
>
> —Anne Lister
> Diarist

Tip 29: Engage Priorities – Be Proactive

You spend your time in certain ways because you choose to do so. Everything you do is through conscious or unconscious choosing. You have the choice to work or not to work; to write that report or not…or to take the phone call or not.

* * * * *

Through conscious planning, you can stay on course in achieving your goals and objectives. Conscious scheduling means being proactive in what, when, how, and where you choose to do those things that are important to you rather than being reactive. *You must take the time to make time. The solution is to focus on the priorities and plan to accomplish them in order of importance.* Otherwise, you may find yourself spending time on trivial matters and less time on those things you consider priorities.

> *The key is not to prioritize what's on your schedule, but to schedule your priorities.*
> —Stephen R. Covey, Author
> *Principle-Centered Leadership*

Tip 30: Offer Praise and Recognition

As a community police leader, if you have people helping you, whether a co-worker or a community volunteer, always offer praise. People are an important part of your success, and by providing praise, recognition, and support in return, they will continue showing dedication and work hard in helping you reach your goals.

* * * * *

When people feel appreciated, they feel good about their efforts, thus their motivational levels will rise. Showing appreciation and respect can inspire you, as a community leader, to put forth more effort. In doing so, you can develop good working relationships because praise influences feelings of joy, satisfaction, well-being, and pride in the work being done.

> *No matter how busy you are, you must take time to offer praise and make the other person feel important.*
> —Mary Kay Ash
> Actor

Tip 31: Don't Be Complacent — Harmful to a Beginner's Mind

A beginner's mind is open, eager, and free from preconceived notions. In reality, we all start off with a beginner's mind! Every time you learn something new, you are in the "*beginner mode.*" Then, what happens to that nimble, open mind down the road?

* * * * *

The moment something becomes familiar to you, your mind attempts to take over, as it calls up memories and thereby creates defeating expectations and fears. In turn, you stop connecting directly to the reality of the present moment and in most instances, take the safe road. It is important to maintain fearlessness and to be available to the moment. *Be spontaneous and disregard the thought of failure by holding onto your beginner's mind.*

> *In the beginner's mind there are many possibilities, but in the expert's there are few.*
>
> —Shunryu Suzuki, Author
> *Zen Mind, Beginner's Mind*

Tip 32: Practice Empathy with Your Job Performance

Study after study has revealed that empathy is positively related to job performance and work ethics. The studies concluded that professionals who show more empathy toward their customers and those that they serve perform better in their fields by far, while empathy boosts stronger relationships, customer satisfaction, and decreases shame.

* * * * *

Most people are naturally empathetic to others (able to understand what someone is feeling and reflect back that understanding). In interpersonal relationships and cross-cultural communities, it helps to deepen rapport and trust. In sensitive areas the lack of empathy toward customs and religious beliefs can alienate customers by creating conflict and shame. Practicing empathy is the perfect counter to these feelings.

Simple Steps to Challenge Yourself and Increase Your Empathy:
- *Activate your listening skills*
- *Fine tune your nonverbal observation skills*
- *Watch TV (drama) with the volume down to practice nonverbal communication*

> *If we can share our story with someone who responds with empathy and understanding, shame can't survive.*
>
> —Brené Brown
> Professor, Author

Chapter 3

Mastery of Attitude Possession

You cannot always control what happens to you, but you can control your attitude toward what happens to you. In that, you will be mastering change rather than allowing it to master you.

—Brian Tracy, Author

Tip 33: Be Happy: It's All About Attitude

Everyone wants to live on top of the mountain, but all the happiness and growth occurs while you're climbing it.

* * * * *

When you began your career as a professional you likely did so because of your desire to help and serve. But, as time moves on, sometimes cynicism or burnout can also be your reality as stress, repetitive work, and challenges in community policing easily exists. These elements are critical to your existence and also to the community and the customers you serve. The professional who's never happy in their work will seemingly manage to find fault with the administration, the public, and even fellow crime fighters. In the "*Us vs. Them*" syndrome it is important that you be mindful of the insulation of your profession and of the continuous struggle to maintain control. Learn ways to embrace a positive mindset and a happy, upbeat attitude. Always remember to take care of yourself first!

> *Happiness and a positive attitude is something, everyone can work on, and everyone can learn how to employ it.*
>
> —Joan Lunde Journalist

Tip 34: Kujichagulia and an Unstoppable Attitude

Develop a winning and unstoppable attitude to achieve success through (*Kujichagulia*) self-determination. You need to have determination. With good intentions, you may find a close friend or co-worker who feels it would be better if you focus your attention in another direction. Don't allow this to sway your attitude and under-ride your determination.

* * * * *

Constable Janeen displayed an unstoppable attitude during her experience with an Indian Nation community that she served. She and the voiceless Indian Nation leadership believed that the many Indian Artifacts on display on a shelf in a corner grocery store in a small Oklahoma township deserved to be part of a display in the shared local town museum. The Indian Nation leaders met resistance from the City Council members and the larger society. But, Constable Janeen's attitude toward the resistance was unstoppable. She reached out and eventually secured a seat at the City Council table for two members of the tribe, who were heard loud and clear. After consideration, the treasured Indian Artifacts had a new home.

> *Move out of your comfort zone. You can only grow if you are willing to feel awkward and uncomfortable when you try something new.*
>
> —Brian Tracy, Author
> *Brian Tracy's 21 Secrets to Success*

Tip 35: By All Means Have Courage

Courage is not the absence of fear, but the acquired ability to move beyond the fear.

* * * * *

Depending on your specific success, it may take courage to arrive at your desired destination in spite of others. You may have a dream of becoming the best community officer in your district because you grew up in that community and you have a level of established success. However, your co-workers may tell you that in-order to grow beyond your current success you will have to, in their minds, "*maintain distance from the people you know and serve.*" Then and only then, they say, will you establish clear leadership in the community. If you understand your purpose and your direction, then having the courage to stand up for what you believe and desire, even if it means negating your co-worker's suggestions is the strategy you must embrace.

> *Efforts and courage are not enough without purpose and direction.*
>
> —John F. Kennedy
> 35th American President

Tips 36: Embrace Your Passion

True passion does not go unnoticed. It is an emotion that comes from within you. True passion is your drive, motivation, and your enthusiasm or excitement. You should dream, create, and live with your passion.

* * * * *

Being passionate means to be invested; to be driven by enthusiasm, limitless motivation, and energy. You need to possess a grounded passion in your work as a community police officer. If you are solidly fixed in your passion and interact successfully with the community you serve, you have complete knowledge of your path, and you have crystal clear insight and peace with your work performance. You should be aware that members of your community will also embrace their passions and you will, however, need to practice patience, as well.

> *The only way to do great work is to love what you do. If you haven't found your passion yet, keep looking. As with all matters of the heart, you'll know when you find it.*
>
> —Steve Jobs,
> CEO & Entrepreneur of Apple Industries

Tip 37: Practice Patience and Perseverance

Your work in community policing is easy in the beginning. It's after you've engaged in the work for some time that you might recognize difficulties and obstacles. When setbacks arise, you must acknowledge that they are not failures. If you take them as failures, you may lose patience and sight of the intended goals and stop moving forward. Maintaining patience and perseverance is important.

* * * * *

The key difference between patience and perseverance is that perseverance indicates an *action* and patience *does not*. Knowing when to embrace either element as you provide customer service in your community is critical to the relationships you have built. Expect to face trials and tribulations, but you should also endure them with patience and perseverance.

> " *Patience and perseverance have a magical effect before which difficulties disappear, and obstacles vanish.*
> —John Quincy Adams
> 6th American President

Tip 38: Define Your Core Values

Core values represent your fundamental beliefs. They are important and essential prioritized steps that serve to guide you as to how you must serve and perform your work. Core values help you to know what is right from wrong. They are not descriptions of the work that you do or the strategies you use to accomplish your mission; rather they underlie the work or the service that you perform.

Five Examples of Core Values:

- *The Delivery of Quality Customer Service Excellence*
- *Doing the Right Thing*
- *The Delivery of Integrity in Your Services*
- *Building Trust and Honest Relationships through Communication*
- *Being Passionate and Determined*

> *Your beliefs become your thoughts. Your thoughts become your words. Your words become your actions. Your actions become your habits. Your habits become your values… Your values become your destiny.*
>
> —Mahatma Ghandi
> Indian Civil Rights Leader

Tip 39: Grasp Humility and Be Thankful

Be thankful for not only your achievements but also grateful for your failures. Being grateful is the art of being humble. People who exhibit this trait not only seek out more success, but they draw success into their lives.

* * * * *

Being humble and grateful draws others around you. You help them to see the positive elements in daily life and to feel more hopeful about the possibility of future success. For example, during community interaction and serving customers, the customers you serve may enjoy feeling that you are grateful for their presence in the community because your actions represent humility. In turn, it can create strong bonds of loyalty and mutual support within the community you serve. Customers are, typically, turned away from bragging, arrogant, and ungrateful people.

> *It is utterly impossible to be successful and happy without being grateful.*
>
> —Toni Sorenson, Author
> *Redemption Road*

Tip 40: Practice Rewarding Yourself

Rewards can be viewed as sources of fuel to keep you on a

new path. When rewards stimulate a positive change, the rewards are used correctly.

* * * * *

If you're stuck in a mental slump, rewarding yourself is a great way to break out of that rut. You can do this by creating new paths or habits through a system of rewards. Celebrating behavior change with rewards recognizes your challenges, motivates and builds self-esteem and self-worth. But first, you must do the work.

As a community policing agent, maybe you've enrolled in a language course that is reflective of the growing population in the community you serve. The language course could be complicated and seemingly overwhelming. However, you would likely see the approval on the faces of your customers if you greeted them in their language. This would be the time to reward yourself for a job well done.

> *All the so-called secrets of success will not work unless you do.*
> — Anonymous

Tip 41: Celebrate Something Every Day

Frequently, our days fly by without us embracing anything that seems to be significant or anything that represents a tangible improvement.

* * * * *

You should make sure that no matter how small the effort, that you will acknowledge your dreams or efforts. You should not wait until you reach accomplishments to be proud of yourself and celebrate. Rather, you should be proud every step of the way and celebrate accordingly.

> *Celebrate continuously, not just once. Every day can be a day to celebrate something. Every day is an opportunity for a reward.*
>
> – Anonymous

Tip 42: Develop Realistic Expectations

"Successful people don't get everything they want, but they do want most of what they get. They make certain that the odds are in their favor by deciding to 'place value' on those things that are within their grasp." —*Anonymous*

* * * * *

People who see success through an evasive lens often set unrealistic expectations and unreasonable goals, thus setting themselves and their actions up for failure. Avoid fantasy expectations of success. Live in the world of reality and strive to make things better, not perfect.

A community policing agent recognized that a slow response time by community police had created distrust and, also, a lack of confidence from the community residents. His intent was to generate a new community perspective. The policing agent considered countering the issue by recommending a decrease in the actual response time by at least 25%. In the interim, he found that this would have been a difficult challenge to fulfill since response time in the area had already been decreased by 10%. The odds would not be favorable for this unrealistic expectation to decrease police response time by an additional 25%. If attempted, excuses would likely prevail as careless goal-setting would create a downward path toward failure and additional disappointment in the community.

> *We expect more of ourselves than we have any right to.*
> —Oliver Wendell Holmes
> Associate Justice of Supreme Court

Tip 43: Practice Personal Tolerance

Tolerance means to recognize and respect the rights, opinions, or practices of others, and to endure. It is a willingness to accept cultural identities, behaviors, and beliefs that are different from your own, even if you disagree with or disapprove of them (*Cambridge English Dictionary*, 2016).

* * * * *

As a community policing agent serving your community, you can learn to be a tolerant servant to the customers you serve by learning personal tolerance through practice. Through careful practice, you may be better able to understand your customers and transform your thinking to positive and meaningful thoughts and action, while being mindful of policing methods and skills.

Tolerance in Non-Threatening Situations:

- *You will not return abuse with abuse, violence with violence, hatred with hatred, or any other negative emotion with a negative one.*
- *You will not react, and you will try your utmost to maintain your state of evenness.*
- *You will repeat the practices until it becomes part of your habits.*

> *You cannot simultaneously cherish peoples' culture while discarding their beliefs.*
>
> —Alex Acutain
> *7 Things to Do Before You Submit Your Screenplay*

Tip 44: Use Your Work Positively

What does work give us? At its best, our work gives us a sense of purpose. Additionally, our professional work allows us the chance to appreciate life and its meaning outside of the workplace.

* * * * *

Sincere appreciation of your work translates into the recognition of those elements that matter. For example, researchers point out that law enforcement jobs are likely one of the most unappreciated jobs by its customers. A lack of appreciation does not mean that those who actually work in community policing should feel the same. Rather, your ability to work in this field, to give back and affect others through your thoughts, ideas, and actions, while developing yourself in the process, is incredibly valuable to your life outside of the workplace.

Knowing that your talents and perspectives are needed, wanted, and unique can provide immense worth and value to you as you commit to your work. Become grateful and appreciative of your job. Take into account what you have and what you give to others, rather than focusing on what you may or may not be receiving.

> *Sometimes, you need those bad work days because it helps you to truly appreciate life and the good ones.*
>
> — Anonymous

Tip 45: Culture Shock? Be Excited and Not Stagnant

In today's world of globalization that includes ethnic groups and cultures, you should effectively address any fears in facing unfamiliarity and culture shock while providing customer service excellence and justice leadership.

* * * * *

Facing feelings of shock, anxiety, and emotional disorientation can be the result of culture shock when community police deal with new cultures and dynamics when providing service. I found this to be a real phenomenon during my international workshops in community police awareness/trainings in Abu Dhabi and Dubai. Culture shock or culture clashing can inhibit the building of effective relationships. In my awareness/trainings, we worked together on three of the primary stages of culture shock and channeled them into feelings of liberation. This included acknowledging the frustrations associated with customs, languages, and the subsequent miscommunications; the practice of adjusting while opening the mind and oneself to feel comfortable; and finally accepting the differences without judging or feeling torn about the cultural differences.

> *You should be against ignorance. You should feel excited that you have to educate yourself, no matter what the situation. People who refuse to educate themselves — people who refuse to understand what others are about, or even what they're frightened of — find comfort in being stagnant and being ignorant.*
>
> —Zeena Schreck and
> Amanda Coleman-Mason,
> President of Adissa Justice Leadership Coaching

Tip 46: Eliminate the Toxic Poisoning

It's not that the whole person is toxic. Rather, their behavior is toxic, or the relationship with the person or group is toxic.

* * * * *

It's common for people with toxic behavior to: create drama in their lives or be surrounded by it; try to manipulate or control others; be jealous and envious of others and bemoan others' happiness and their own bad misfortune. If you are serious about reaching your goals and being successful, you may need to eliminate these people from your circle.

Recognize the Signs of Toxic Poisoning:
- *You are emotionally affected by their drama*
- *You dread (or fear) being around them*
- *You ignore your values*
- *You feel sorry or ashamed of yourself*
- *You have feelings of being controlled*

> *When poison words are spoken by others, do not swallow the poison.*
>
> —June Davidson
> President of ASLA

Tip 47: Surround Yourself with Like Minds

Your environment shapes who you are, what you do, and who you will become. You're in total control of the choices you make, so why not place yourself in an active and engaging environment that befits your needs.

* * * * *

Select a role model or mentor who motivates and inspires you to stay focused on your goals. Look to an Action Coach to challenge and support you in your direction. Start networking with successful career-oriented people who share similar dreams, or individuals who have already done what you're doing. Surround yourself with the thinkers and the listeners; the people who want to set a change and leave a footprint in their lives and yours; the ones who are willing to help others before helping themselves. Listen to their stories; you'll probably learn a thing or two.

> *Keep away from people who try to belittle your ambitions. Small people always do that, but the great make you feel that you too, can become great. Hang out with friends who are like-minded and who are also designing purpose-filled lives.*
>
> —Mark Twain, Author
> *Tom Sawyer*

Tip 48: Be Positive and Be Passionate… It's Healthy

How positive and passionate are you about your work? Do you find yourself feeling reluctant or anxious about going to work every day? Being a community police agent is a highly demanding job, and there are likely many factors that may affect how you feel about the work that you do.

* * * * *

Holding on to negative thoughts and feelings for extended periods of time can make it difficult to support and maintain positive attitudes. You must shift from negative to positive by being conscious of your "self-talk." Ruling out negative thinking can be accomplished by repeating positive comments to yourself several times a day as it can ultimately offer stimulation and health benefits.

* * * * *

Health Benefits of a Positive Attitude:
- *Increases life span*
- *Lowers rates of depression*
- *Lowers levels of distress*
- *Creates better psychological and physical well-being*
- *Reduces risk of death from cardiovascular disease*
- *Creates better coping skills during hardships and stressful time*

> *When careers, passions, and active attitudes blend, it is a beautiful sight.*
> —Amanda Coleman-Mason
> President of Adissa Justice Leadership Coaching

Tip 49: Focus On Solutions

We all approach our problems in different ways, either because that is the way we've always done it, or we find comfort in the process we've chosen. How we focus on our problems has all to do with the results we desire.

* * * * *

Most individuals focus on the problem or the reason why a problem exists (problem-focused thinking). Unknowingly, the problem-focused approach is commonly applied in our everyday life when we have to face a challenging task or when performing certain duties. This type of problem thinking does not necessarily help us in solving difficult situations. When we continue to dwell on the analysis of a problem and fail to "flip the switch" to focusing on a solution, we can become the victim of "analysis paralysis," and thereby delay or miss the opportunity to find an effective solution to an existing problem. As a community policing agent this could have impact on your ability to gain the trust and respect of the community membership you serve.

> *Problem talk creates problems.*
> *Solution talk creates solutions.*
> —Steve de Shazer, Author
> *Patterns of Brief Therapy*

Tip 50: Select Strengths vs. Flaws
Consider what strengths you'll find, if you are looking for your flaws. How many will you find or invent?

* * * * *

On the other hand, if you look for your strengths, how many flaws will you find? And how would your life change in the process? For instance, your police department is beginning a new program within a rapidly changing school district, and they've made the requirements known for the new Youth Liaison Officer position. When you review the list, you concentrate on what you perceive to be your flaws instead of looking at your strengths, such as your bilingual abilities and your athletic skills that could be instrumental in developing a rapport with the multicultural groups of teenagers. Your lack of foresight could cost you an opportunity to grow in your personal development and to expand your capacity to serve your community.

> *From the cradle to the cubicle we devote more time to our shortcomings than our strengths.*
> —Tom Rath, Author
> *Well-being: The Essential Elements*

Tip 51: Treat Individuals As a Person and Not a Stereotype

Stereotyping often goes far beyond race and gender. It can also include national origin, color, and religion as the basis for unfair generalizations. These generalizations can impact both customer service excellence and how you create fairness in your practice of justice leadership.

* * * * *

Stereotyping includes statements about others from certain generations' different philosophical views and discriminatory practices. These are fixed prejudgments and impressions that have little factual meaning. People unwilling to look more deeply into the matter are likely the perpetrators. In cross-cultural communities, these challenges exist in the practice of effective community policing and customer service excellence. It is time to examine your perception of others and the behavior you may exhibit.

In a small community in Racine, Wisconsin, a seasoned female community police agent led a successful youth mentoring project in an after-school program. She was paired with a teenage girl, whom she had never met before. The teenager also happened to be of Asian appearance. Upon meeting her, the officer quipped, *"you're smart…you should be mentoring me."* A confused look crossed the teenager's face. At that precise moment, the community police agent had unconsciously repeated a commonly embraced stereotype concerning Asian intelligence. The impact of the statement was the loss of possibly building a successful interpersonal relationship with this community member. Train your brain to stop snap-judging people by their most obvious attributes. Undoing snap judgment takes time, but it is possible by focusing on the "*unobvious*." Review the challenge and train your brain to move in the right direction.

The Challenge:

- Darken the room. View the picture of irregular black and white shapes.
- Concentrate on the four small dots in the vertical row in the middle of the picture for a minimum of 30
- seconds.
- Then close your eyes and tilt your head back. Keep them closed. With head still tilted back, open your eyes. Eventually, you will see a circle of light.
- Continue looking at the circle. What do you see?

by Michael Michalko

By altering your attention in a different way (focusing on the dots and closing your eyes), you've trained your brain to view something that you perceive as different and then allow yourself to see something that you could not otherwise see.

> " *It's not what you look at that matters;
> it's what you see.*
>
> —Henry David Thoreau,
> Author, Abolitionist, Historian

Tip 52: View Your Job As a Positive Force

Your customers are likely to be very intuitive and they would very much like for you to be "yourself." If you are a straightforward type person, you may have noticed that you occasionally offend others, unknowingly.

* * * * *

As a community police agent, your direct style of interaction within your community can be a disadvantage in today's working environment. No one likes unhappy or aggressive people, who wield their job like a knife; it is a communication blocker. Positively viewing your work and your profession may keep important and significant relationships productive.

Display Positive Forces:
- *Only use positive words when talking*
- *Push out all feelings that aren't positive*
- *Use words that evoke strength and success*
- *Consider your thoughts and be clear*

> *In order to carry a positive action,
> we must develop here a positive vision.*
> —Dalai Lama
> *How to See Yourself as You Are*

Tip 53: Your Contagious Attitude

Your attitude, be it positive or negative, can be contagious. When cultures are different, expect that you may have a subtle yet, powerful impact on the interpersonal relationship you would like to develop.

* * * * *

You want to be noticed for your efforts. It is important to understand that the type of attitude you reveal to those you aspire to embrace in a successful interpersonal relationship is contagious and even infectious. In other words, what you put forth, you will also receive in return.

> *Our attitude towards others
> determines their attitude towards us.*
> —Earl Nightingale, Author, and Speaker
> *Think and Grow Rich*

Tip 54: Ujima[5]: Collectivity & Global Citizenry

Your movement toward building relationships and collective works through communication rests on your ability to understand the impact of your attitudes when interacting with different cultural groups. Culture is the sum of attitudes, customs, and beliefs that distinguish one group of people from another (*Merriam Webster*).

* * * * *

Your ability to understand that all culture is manifested and transmitted in many ways through language, material objects, rituals, institutions, and art, and handed down from one generation to the next is important. Culture becomes who we are. You can use this understanding to build relationships and thereby, build the community you serve in its collective work. It is through this understanding of cultural differences that we get to respect our likenesses, as well as the differences between us as people. Transferring this knowledge to your work as a community police agent assists you in your communication in being capable of building successful relationships and in developing yourself as a global citizen who engages in strengthening collective community work.

> *To become a true global citizen, one must abandon all notions of "otherness" and instead embrace togetherness.*
> —Suzy Kassem, Author
> *Rise Up and Salute the Sun: The Writings of Suzy Kassem*

Tip 55: Examine Your Interactive Reflections

How you treat others may truly be a reflection of you and the way you look at the world. And how you treat others may also be a reflection of how you feel about life and your life, as a whole.

* * * * *

A person who is never content or happy with life or someone who believes that nothing is ever good enough is likely to be a person who treats other people badly. Their discontentment with life makes it possible for them to be discontent with everyone else as they transfer their life attitude. This attitude can be a noticeable problem. You may not think others notice, but they do. In fact, you may believe that the problem is everyone else. But in reality, it is in all liklihood that the problem is *you*!

You are the only one in control of you. If you encounter, say 30 people over time, and it appears to you that they are always out to get you, wouldn't it make more sense to think perhaps that "*it might be you and your attitude*"? In this instance, after all, you are the one common denominator who is involved in every problematic situation.

You must know that if you go out into the world looking for a fight, there will be an argument that you created all by yourself! If you change your thoughts and change your words to others, you will find that people will start to respond differently to you. The way people act towards you is a direct reflection of how you feel about yourself and how you, in turn, make others feel while in your presence.

> *People will forget what you said, people will forget what you did, but people will never forget how you made them feel.*
> —Maya Angelou, Author
> *On the Pulse of Morning*

Tip 56: Maintain Dignity in Cultural Differences

All of us are worthy just because we exist (K. Schneider). Dignity is our legitimate birthright. Dignity is the quality of worth and honor that every human being is owed and cultural differences have absolutely no impact on this human right, even in the eye of power, wealth, and dominance.

* * * * *

Indignity, which is the intentional trespassing or violation of another person's legitimate birthright is the essence of insult, humiliation, and the ultimate root of shame, anger, and hate. In your community as a justice leader, it is your obligation to abstain from this injustice and to demonstrate community and customer respect concerning the legitimacy of each person encountered in your communal relationship circle.

> " *Never take a person's dignity: it is worth everything to them, and nothing to you.*
> -Fran Barron, Pioneer in Psychology

Tip 57: Recognize and Respond

Recognize that you will and must extend energy in planning. But, also recognize that when challenges and obstacles appear to be seemingly insurmountable, you should go into *response* mode by adjusting and transitioning your energy in light of the option of flight or fleeing!

* * * * *

When you want to succeed, you cannot afford to disengage

or retreat. Because retreating is mentally damaging, it is also admitting to failure. If you truly believed that you could realize your dreams, then you won't be tempted by the thought of fleeing. If you find yourself at the crossroads of a fight, when faced with a challenge, it's okay to be afraid. Rather than fight or retreat, one alternative is to stay focused on the path and the direction of your goal.

During meaningful program development, fight or flight may exist. Officer Crandall in Maui, Hawaii, implemented his dream program that provided activities directly related to accelerating youth self-esteem and development in the community. The program hit a snag as youth interests in the program abruptly dropped. Rather than lower the achievement requirements to maintain favorable statistics on youth involvement and completion, Officer Crandall brought in a high-profile local sports figure, who immediately offered group mentoring and role modeling for teens. Not giving up when challenged, or taking a short cut proved to be the response that saved the integrity, value, and promise of Officer Crandall's joint community program.

> *There are no secrets to success. It is the result of preparation, hard work and learning from failure.*
> — Anonymous

Chapter 4

Mastery of Goal Setting

People with clearly written goals accomplish far more in a shorter period than people without them could ever imagine.
—Brian Tracy, Author
Change Your Thinking, Change Your Life

Tip 58: Set Clear Goals

You set goals because you want to see some degree or type of change in your life. Setting goals helps you to separate what is important and what isn't. Goals can prioritize and assist you in creating certainty. And getting certainty out of goals matters as you focus and build confidence in knowing you want to achieve. Focusing on your efforts can be managed through SMART goal techniques. This concept can be reassuring in that you "soundly" identify your goals by utilizing the following criteria: *S=specificity; M=measurable; A=achievable; R=relevant*; and *T=time bound.*

* * * * *

You should know that the primary focus of a goal should be that it stimulates and motivates you. Make certain that the goals you choose are important to you and that there is value in achieving them as your interest in the outcome of your goals is *uniquely relevant to the effort you put forth.* The odds of success are considerably reduced unless you state what you want and understand why you want it in the first place. Commit to the SMART concept to increase and maximize your probability of success.

> *If you aim at nothing, you will hit it every time.*
> —Zig Ziglar, Author
> *Zig Ziglar's Leadership and Success*

Tip 59: Are Your Goals Reachable, Timely?

It goes without saying, that if you want to succeed, then you must set goals. Even though you may know that you need to set goals, do you know how to set effectively reachable goals; that is, goals that are achievable?

* * * * *

In most instances, when we seek success we want those results to come to us overnight. However, expecting overnight success is not realistic. Rather, you will need to examine and analyze your goals to determine a realistic time. In order to maintain practical and achievable goals for yourself it's been suggested that you re-evaluate your goals from time to time. If functional changes are not useful, you will likely become frustrated and quit.

> *Your goal should be just out of reach,
> but not out of sight.*
> —Denis Waitley and Remi Witt

Tip 60: Take Advantage of Goal-Oriented Training

The practice of goal-oriented training programs has grown in popularity among professional organizations. These types of trainings focus on the *"end results or outcomes of the tasks instead of the tasks themselves."* Their purpose in community policing is to train competent, ethical, and reflective community police agents who have acquired the soft skills that include awareness, knowledge, understanding, and efficient communication. Goal-oriented training is an enhancement mechanism for seasoned professionals with a focus toward core goals and values as well as outcomes.

An *"experienced"* police firearms instructor will tell you that they can accomplish more with 50 rounds of ammunition while doing a ball and dummy drill, than just burning up hundreds of rounds by blowing holes in paper. It's not so much *what* you do that's important ,but *why* you do it and the results you achieve!

How to Achieve Your Goal:

- *Define it!*
- *Write it down!*
- *Believe it!*
- *Split it up!*
- *Review it!*
- *Make it happen!*
- *Examine the results!*

> *Keep working towards your goals.*
> *Take it day by day.*
> *Focus on the results and outcomes.*
>
> —Molly Tumblr
> Illustrator

Tip 61: Align Your Goals with One Another

Step back and ask the bigger question: *"What do you want out of life?"* Is it essential to your personal goal development? It is critical that you make sure your personal and professional goals are compatible with your desired outcomes.

* * * * *

What if the four tires on your car were not aligned correctly? The likelihood is that your car would not steer or move in the direction that you desired. Goals work the same way. They must all be aligned toward the same results to make progress in the same direction. Keeping your behavior in alignment with your goals requires that you be deliberate and purposeful in your action.

> *The key is not to prioritize what's on your schedule but to synchronize your priorities.*
>
> —Steven R. Covey, Author
> *The Leader in Me*

Tip 62: Visualize Yourself in Your Goals

Some people are great at visualizing the goals they set as well; there are others who are not aware of visualization techniques. Visualizing your goals is a useful method that sharpens and engages the mind in a natural step-by-step process. In other words, it is the process of seeing your projected achievement through your "*mind's eye.*"

* * * * *

If you are capable of visualizing a goal, then you've come to realize that it is not a complicated process as you become "*one*" with your original dream. As you see yourself in your goal, your goal will deepen, your desire will become heightened, and you will ultimately see yourself taking the necessary actions to make it happen. A great example of this is a community police officer in upstate New York, who served residents in a multi-cultural community. This community also had a youth population that was proportionately higher than its older residents. The officier recognized that youths appeared to be more restless during the school term than from the previous year. At the same time, the athletic officer envisioned a vacant lot as a soccer field for the teens. He also persuaded some of the older, agile residents to interact with the teens as coaches and mentors. He engaged the elders in meetings and plans, and within three months, the community was able to clear and landscape the vacant lot to begin competitive matches between community teams, just in time for the summer.

If you struggle with visualizations, possibly you've not discovered your actual mindset type. In the following challenge, you can determine your mindset and have a better understanding as to whether your mindset is a "*fixed*" *focus* or a "*growth*" *focus*. It can reveal how you deal with setbacks, achievements, and how you visualize and set your goals.

The Challenge:

Use the first finger of your dominant hand to trace the capital letter "Q" on your forehead. Trace the letter "Q" on your forehead with the tail of Q toward your right eye or with the tail toward your left eye (as in the illustration below).

Results: Tail to the left: A *"fixed"* mindset that focuses outwardly and is stagnant about personal abilities and abilities of others. You offer external reasons for failures or lack of achievement. It is difficult to take personal responsibility for mistakes or failures. and you focus on actual and low-risk experiences.

Tail to the right: A *"growth"* mindset that focuses inwardly and can be developed, as high achievement comes from hard work, dedication, and persistence in meeting goals. You tend to focus on internal controls such as beliefs, and attitudes with no regards toward social circumstances.

> *Focus and visualize your goals, as if it has already been reached. Make it real in your mind, and you will soon make it a reality.*
>
> —Anonymous

Tip 63: Give Up Your Morals for Your Goals?

While seeking success, you may have found yourself in conflict with the goals that you set as a measurement of achievement and your morals. If your standards of behavior and the goals you set are in conflict, your success may not be achievable. Through self-evaluation and identification of the standards of behavior that you embrace, the two should align succinctly in achieving success.

* * * * *

A once-prominent pharmaceutical CEO developed a drug that would halt the advancement of Sickle Cell Anemia for 4-10 years. The life-threatening disease primarily affects African Americans. The CEO noted that this phenomenal medication would elevate the time line of the company's goal in achieving its success by 10-12 years.

However, the medication came with a serious flaw in which the individual taking the drug could conceivably become sterile after 6-8 years of consuming it. Just before the release of the report on the medication, the CEO pulled the application for government trials citing the worthiness of the drug. He could not justify or sacrifice his moral value for the monetary success he would have achieved.

> *When you have to compromise yourself or your morals for the goals you've chosen, it's probably time to change your goals.*
>
> —Anonymous

Tip 64: Share Your Success

As you arrive at the end of your process, and your success has come to light, don't stop there. *Rejoice in your victory!* It is important that you also, take the next step and share your success by using your experience to teach, guide, or mentor another.

* * * * *

Share the concept of mentoring. In doing so, you will be providing a less experienced colleague in your law enforcement community an opportunity to engage and become anchored in the skills and techniques that may offer an opportunity for them to succeed. Sharing and mentoring will promote the *sharer's* professional growth, inspire them in their motivation, and increase the effectiveness of their community relations and customer service excellence.

> *Each one, teach one.*
> —African-American Slave Proverb

Chapter 5
Mastery of Community and Customer Service Excellence Skills

The challenge that many people face when interacting with others is that they lack the necessary interpersonal skills needed to be effective.

—Robert W. Lucas, Author
Customer Service Skills for Success

Tip 65: Understand Community Policing

Community policing stresses prevention, early identification, and timely intervention to deal with issues before they become unwieldy problematic.

* * * * *

Community-based police departments recognize that policing agents *cannot adequately address all matters alone*. The concept of community policing means that police must realize that a steadfast community partnership must exist, as they share a mutual responsibility for resolving community concerns, problems, and situations while creating customer service excellence.

> *I am in favor of community policing because it builds
> better working relationships within the community.*
> —Vincent Frank
> Political Activist

Tip 66: Know the Community Leadership

You need to know and understand the community [customers] you serve, particularly the leaders and organizers of the community, when creating customer service excellence.

* * * * *

It is important that you know and work with the leaders in your diverse community. Even if you are not directly involved in the customer service business, there is one clear action that you can employ to please your customers, and that is to "*act like serving them is your very first priority.*"

Given the national upheaval concerning policing since Ferguson, MO, importance has been lifted in regards to the level of trust between community members and police departments. One primary reflection of community leadership concerns community police agents' willingness to never dismiss anyone's negative experiences with the police, what they've gone through, or what their loved ones have gone through. This one action alone implies the offering of respect and dignity to the community and its leadership.

> *Listening to feedback makes customers feel more appreciated and part of the value creation process.*
> —Ray Poynter, Author
> *The Handbook of the Noble Market*

Tip 67: Attract Your Community with Customer Service Excellence

Your mission and core values must speak to and attract the community [customers] you serve as you perform community policing. You should be willing to provide customer service excellence. In other words, *"give your community members more service than they expect or anticipate."*

The customer needs to understand the sincere intent of your work. Your combined knowledge of the community and the community's knowledge of you will attract the community to you.

> *Respect is earned. Honesty is appreciated.*
> *Trust is gained. Loyalty is returned.*
> *Customers expect the same.*
>
> —Anonymous

Tip 68: Be Involved in Your Community

The philosophy of community policing is a strategy based on partnership and the interactions of law enforcement with the community. It acts as a detour to possible crime-related problems, and it allows the community to feel safe.

* * * * *

In some deeply divided cross-cultural societies where minorities live in segregated communities, cultural codes can conflict with the dominant majority, especially with regards to informal social controls. Community policing, by its very nature, can be a complex task. In this case, the minority group may feel vulnerable and hesitant about contacting the community police. Ignoring the impact of cultural differences is not an option as the minority community's perception of the police may be negative and lead to distrust and unchecked crime. Be involved!

> *Taking the time to build community, to get to know your people will have long-lasting benefits.*
> —Clifton Taulbert, Author
> *The Last Train North*

Tip 69: Make Opportunities for Interaction

Take advantage of possibilities to increase police and community relations. Rather than wait for an opportunity to find you, you should practice being proactive in finding opportunities to interact with the customers you serve.

* * * * *

Be aware of community needs and the problems in the community you serve, as you may have something beneficial to present or discuss, perhaps at the next Common Council meeting. For example, a council meeting is planned to discuss how the community should proceed as they address traffic lights in a busy school zone that has caused anxiety for the parents and students. Ask the leader of the event if you can be present at the meeting to offer possible solutions from your professional [police] expertise.

> *Opportunities are like sunrises.*
> *If you wait too long, you miss them.*
> —William Arthur Ward, Writer
> *Inspirational Words of Wisdom*

Tip 70: Develop a "We" — "Umoja" Mentality

Skills and techniques are essential in providing excellent service to customers, but they aren't the only keys to successfully engaging in customer service excellence. Developing a *"we"* mentality means *unity* (*Umoja*) in the face of challenges and mistakes.

* * * * *

When situations arise, it could be easy to blame your fellow officers or the persons you work with on a day-to-day basis, as they are most likely the closest to you. As the challenges in community policing and providing effective customer service in the community can be stressful and demanding, it is important that you do not develop divisive thoughts and verbiage. Words can hurt, and they can be difficult to let go of when someone on your team says something like: *"You made a mistake!"* Rather than use this type of language, use language that promotes bonding, while working through challenges. Using language like: *"We can get through this"* allows you to focus on a solution and not the problem. The impact of this tip is intense, particularly, when community policing agents must be aware of the necessity of unity and trust among fellow officers and the community.

> *I believe that if you show people the problem and then you show them the solution they will be moved to act.*
>
> —Bill Gates
> *Microsoft Entrepreneur*

Tip 71: Create Value by Focusing on Customer Service Excellence

Your organization's primary focus should squarely rest on exceeding the expectations of your customers or clients.

* * * * *

As leaders in community policing, you should engage in a helping culture whereby you and your co-workers wholeheartedly embrace your customer's needs and wants. *The real value of your organization is tied directly to the future and your highly satisfied and loyal customers.* The focus should be on the community you serve and in addressing their problems, needs, and concerns. It should not be about your organizational structure, political affiliations, or revenues. The value is to help and serve your customers, serve them well, and sniff out any customer problems or complaints in the community as soon as possible.

You create value in your community by focusing on the customers you serve. *Keeping your customers delighted, feeling respected and valued should be your primary focus!*

> "*I will heighten my life by helping others strengthen theirs.*
>
> —Les Brown
> Motivational Speaker

Tip 72: Be Efficient in Giving Excellent Service

Being efficient and providing customer service excellence is a huge challenge for service-minded entities such as fire and protection, as well as community policing. However, the drive for efficiency can ultimately impact the efforts in providing customer service excellence.

While in pursuit of keeping close to budgets, service delivery by community policing can be influenced. As is the case in such budget restraints, services may become mechanistic or scripted rather than focused on the cultural dynamics of the community being served. Using a "*one method*" style of interacting with the community may be efficient, but the risk is that the customer may not feel that they are valued. Consumers of community policing are not generic, and it is critical that community policing efforts recognize it. It is best to respond with flexibility to the needs and culture of the community, and yet be flexible and diverse in your servant leadership.

> *People expect good service,*
> *but few are willing to give it.*
>
> —Robert Gately
> Campbell Corporation Executive

Tip 73: Cultural Differences in Delivering Customer Service Excellence

Customer Service Excellence is a strategy that begins with understanding the group that you work with and then going beyond their expectations of service.

* * * * *

When working with an unfamiliar group or a culture that is different from your own, your job in providing customer service excellence can be a series of small challenges and changes. It is critical that you recognize that there is value in appreciating cultural differences in the community while working in unison toward a common goal. Acknowledge your perceptions in the cultural differences while delivering your services. But, be available to also discuss the differences, as the customer (member of the community) and you, can look at the same situation or concern and see something different. Review the challenge.

The Challenge:

> *Coming together is a beginning. Keeping together is progress. Working together is the success.*
> —Henry Ford
> Auto Maker

Tip 74: Identifying Quality Customer Service Excellence

Quality service satisfies customer needs, real or perceived, in a consistent and dependable manner. It's not your perception as a community policing agent as to how good the service is that counts. It's the customer's perception of the service and those who depend on it that counts.

Providing Quality:

- *Acknowledge customer discontent quickly.*
- *Seek to fix the mistakes and misunderstandings.*
- *Go the extra mile.*

- *Think long-term.*
- *Know the customers you serve.*

> *The quality of our service depends on the knowledge and the quality of our people who serve.*
> —Anonymous

Tip 75: Kujichagulia: Be Self-Determined and Open to New Ideas

It is essential to your continuous success and insight to never stop learning and adapting.

* * * * *

Your work in community policing and relationship building will always change, as will the people and the situations you may encounter. Success is related to your *self-determination* (*Kujichagulia*) in never becoming complacent or unwilling to learn new strategies or ideas in your work strengthends your confidence and judgment.

Patrolman Ernesto, who worked in a San Bernadino barrio, suffered from situational complacency or a lack of self-determination in growing. In other words, he slacked off in his work and he allowed fellow officers to assume a portion of his community work. At one point he had begun to feel inadequate due to a gradual influx of culturally different residents in the community. He had not grasped changes that the vibrant community members presented. His problem was his lack of self-determination and insight related to the new cultural dynamics of the community. Ultimately, the outcome could present adverse impact on his ability to build relationships with new community residents.

> *The secret of change is to focus all of your energy, not on fighting the old, but on building and learning the new.*
>
> —Socrates, Philosopher

Tip 76: Trust in Community Policing Creates Customer Service Excellence

The greatest indication of success with any outreach initiative involving community policing and customer service excellence occurs when you have the ability to recognize residents who actually reach out and get involved because they *"trust community policing."* These actions are never truer than with cross-cultural community members.

* * * * *

When police in a densely populated northern Hispanic community in Baltimore, MD, received a call from a young Latina mother, the community police were encouraged that their police interactions had established a level of mutual respect. This mother stated that she trusted the police department because of the work being done by police at the neighborhood park, which had been engaging the community and seeking residential feedback. The communication from this Latina mother was encouraging to the department as the much-needed resources were provided to the community.

> *Trust is the glue of life. It's an essential ingredient in effective communication. It's the foundational principle that holds all relationships together.*
>
> —Stephen R. Covey, Author
> Habit# Synergize

Tip 77: Neighborhood Partnering

Suburbs, cities, and rural areas host healthy neighborhoods and communities alike. While some communities host active sectors that support thriving businesses, others may struggle with relative issues and concerns related to their identity and cultural dynamics and their social resources. Your role in community policing can offer an active part in developing community collaborations.

* * * * *

As some communities face difficulties, challenges, economic problems, and crime, the unchecked tensions between different groups may become strained even more when members do not know each other. If allowed to progress, this lack of awareness can become increasingly problematic when new residents with cultural differences become part of the neighborhood. Community policing can serve a role in unified partnering and collaborations that ultimatey build trust.

Neighborhood Partnering and Collaborations:

- *Assist families in opening up to talk about their experiences*
- *Assist families in feeling that they are a part of the larger community*
- *Assist in open neighborhood focus and discussions in understanding members of the community*
- *Assist families in taking pride in their own cultures and identities*

> *We should not be defined by what we extract from our community. We will be defined by what we give to our community.*
>
> —Anonymous

Tip 78: The Right Support Team and Residency Training

It is easy to take others' support for granted. You may have friends or colleagues that you vent to about work when you've had a bad day or week. But in the day-to-day interaction with your community and in creating customer service excellence, how do you intentionally bring others *"under the tent"* in your quest to grow as an active community policing agent?

* * * * *

As a self-aware and seasoned community policing agent, you should recognize that you need to rethink your support system consistently. Most of us intuitively know the value of having a support group for changing our habits, learning new things, or achieving new work-related goals. Real and earnest leadership, management, and a devoted team of co-workers to assist you in being successful in your work is extremely valuable and beneficial. In turn, as a seasoned community policing agent, you can provide and offer leadership as a mentor during Residency Training. This consistent training provides an opportunity for new community policing agents to interact with the community as they apply their technical skills and their self-development skills in real time. Newly committed policing agents can be brought "under the tent" as they use their self-development skills in the community they serve.

> *"Alone we can do so little;*
> *together we can do so much.*
> —Helen Heller
> American Author, Lecturer

Tip 79: Review International Policing Collaborations

The concept of International Collaborative exchanges in learning environments (community policing) has become a growing endeavor in police training and coaching, nationally, as well as internationally.

* * * * *

Rapid community changes over past decades, particularly in the 21st century, has ushered in an abundance of knowledge-led policing and collaborative efforts. Police teaching institutions now find it beneficial to expand the reservoir of learning resources. In Hong Kong a revision of the Police College vision to further develop police integrity and to better serve Hong Kong's international and multicultural communities is being pushed, through various additional training. Similarly, the Abu Dhabi Police Dept. in the UAE, of which I consulted with and trained some of its community policing force, has also adopted knowledge-led policing revisions. Both country's revisions in training are rooted in broadly based analysis, decision making, critical focus, and learning principles as related to community collaboration and inclusivity (Ratcliff, J.).

> *"Genuine collaboration is an environment*
> *that promotes communication, learning,*
> *maximum contribution and innovation.*
> —Jane Ripley, Author
> *Collaboration Begins with You: Be a Silo Buster*

Tip 80: Umoja: School Collaborations

When community policing plans significantly enhance relationships with students, parents, and school staff, it ultimately creates unity (*Umoja*) and positive impact on the community. Success begins with unity.

* * * * *

Today, community policing collaborations with youth appear to be on the rise. Community collaborative (*Umoja*) efforts strive to be inclusive in the lives of children and young people. In cross-cultural communities, these efforts in pursuing educational opportunities provide a voice for those community members, who may feel silent and invisible. When community policing agents form partnerships, and collaborate and communicate with diverse communities on the educational goals and attainment for the children and youth of its diverse community, the results can have an impact in such areas as school truancy and other outlying issues.

> *Collaboration is the essence of life. The wind, bees, and flowers work together, to spread the pollen. Mindfulness gives us the opportunity to work with the cosmic collaboration.*
>
> —Amit Ray, Author
> *Mindfulness: Living in the Moment – Living in the Breath*

Tip 81: Choose Triumph vs. Trying

In many ways, you and you alone are responsible for your success as you dig deep into understanding others and in being heard, as well, in the community you serve. In most instances, your responsibility lies in your pursuit and your efforts. But, at some point, the achievement should become your focal point as the triumph is within reach.

* * * * *

Triumph or Victory is evident when the adversity, challenge, or obstacle is no longer apparent, and you feel good about the efforts that you have put forth. Choose to be joyous over the difficulties or challenges that you encountered as a community policing agent. The reward for your steadfast commitment and application of soft skills in developing interpersonal relationships ultimately assist you in embracing your goals and achievement.

> *"Embrace your thoughts of triumph over your mediocre ideas of "trying." The difference between "try" and "triumph" is just a little "umph."*
> —Bonnie Pryzybyski,
> Projects Manager W.R. Grace

Tip 82: Embrace Your Social Engagement

Finding ways for effective community policing translates to actively giving back to your community through respectful social engagement.

* * * * *

With recent media reports and stories regarding unfortunate incidents between communities and law enforcement, sometimes the focus on these incidences can paint a negative or unfair picture of policing or community policing agents. These can lead to a misplaced loss of trust by the public. However, socially aware departments develop successful programs that attempt to involve the interaction of police with members of the communities. In most cases, officer's face-to-face interaction is vital to the success of social engagement programs. The most popular socially engaged programs include Crime Prevention and Police/Youth Interaction programs. In these programs, you can facilitate honest and open interactions between the community and yourself, while adhering to the standards of mutual respect and a commitment to address the problems and concerns that may exist within community partnerships and expectations.

> " *The best way to address engagement is to sit in the community space and listen.*
> —Dr. Iris Iwanicki
> Planning Institute of Australia, CEO

Tip 83: Practice Self-Care

While practicing self-care may seem overly simplistic, it requires mentioning. Of course, you've adhered to the physical regiments and requirements of your profession, but have you sought to keep your mental capacities as fine-tuned?

Often, mental sharpness is not a prominent thought process as we pursue our daily work. Can you and do you let go? On a daily basis, you see, hear, and speak about the concerns of the members of the community you serve. A typical outcome of the dedicated work that you perform as a community policing agent can be Compassion Fatigue. In this instance, you allow your community police work to "*shape your life,*" as disengaging is sometimes difficult.

* * * * *

Strategies that you can engage in include the practice of

self-talk. Self-talk can be used to remind yourself that you are not in your police vehicle when you are sitting in your car. Or remind yourself what is important in life by taking out a family photo. Find a professional or someone you trust and respect to talk about your feelings. Ultimately, you are in charge, and you are likely to be the first to recognize a change. Consider taking steps to keep you whole and in good health.

> " *Self-care is not selfish.*
> *You cannot "serve others" from an empty vessel.*
> —Eleanor Brown, Author
> *The Light of Paris*

Tip 84: Create Opportunities for Openness in Customer Service

In many cases, individuals wait for opportunities to seek them out, rather than identifying and creating the opportunity firsthand.

* * * * *

Community police officers who have had success in gaining community trust and enhanced customer relationships will tell you that they looked for ideas and ways to seize opportunities to partner with the community they serve. In a community in southern Oregon, the crime rate had been slowly rising when it reached a startling 12% overall increase. As community police and officials met with members of the community to solicit input and feedback, they created opportunities that included several internal committees and public participation. Decisions to solicit vocal community dialogue and contributions resulted in a 5% decrease in crimes from the previous year.

> *Without a sense of developing opportunities and voice for the community, there can be no sense of community.*
>
> —Anonymous

Tip 85: Identify Barriers to Enabling Openness in Customer Service Excellence

Community police often come face-to-face with cultural insensitivity when attempting to gain trust and develop effective customer relationships. You can maintain the essential elements of openness and flexibility in gaining community trust by taking steps to counter cultural insensitivities.

* * * * *

Countering Barriers to Customer Service Excellence:

- *Do not allow your emotional reactions to negate the value of those who have cultural differences from you.*
- *Acknowledge your inherited biases openly so that you can listen to those you serve in the community.*
- *Understand that experiences with people of color will enhance your cultural competency (knowledge).*
- *Do not shut down when faced with dissent or disagreement.*
- *Take an active role in knowing yourself.*

> *If you talk to a man in a language he understands, that goes to his head. If you talk to him in his language, that goes to his heart.*
>
> —Nelson Mandela
> Former South African President

Chapter 6

Mastery of Communication and Effective Listening

The Precision of communication is important, more important than ever, in our era of hair-trigger balances, when a false or misunderstood word may create as much disaster as a sudden thoughtless act.
—James Thurber, Author, Actor
Conversations with Thurber

Tip 86: Know Your High and Low Context in Communication

Do you tend to let your words speak for themselves, or do you prefer to be less direct, relying solely on what was implied through your communication (*low-context communication*)? Or do you prefer indirect verbal communication from others? Or are you attuned to a whole range of verbal and nonverbal cues to help you understand the meaning of what is said (*high-context communication*)?

* * * * *

We all engage in both high-context and low-context communication. For example, we may at times *"say what we mean and mean what we say"* leaving almost no room for guessing *"as others read into"* an uncomplicated message. Direct communication represents low-context communication. The opposite applies when we may infer, imply, insinuate, or deliver the message with nonverbal cues without actually speaking the words. Indirect communication aligns with high-context communication.

We know when to be direct and clear and when it is best to embrace messages that spare feelings or avoid confrontation. However, when cultural languages, manners, and regions of ethnic origin dictate how communication is projected (*high or low context*), we may find ourselves in conflict within a multi-cultural community if we are not aware of the strategies and dynamics of cultural patterns. As a learned and conscious community policing agent, your charge is to handily determine the balance of nonverbal and direct communications. Listen with care and purpose in understanding the dynamics and strategies of communication from those you serve.

> *I see and hear things not as they are but, as they might be.*
>
> —Anonymous

Tip 87: Know the Differences Between Listening and Hearing

The quality of your interactive work in community policing is primarily based on your hearing and listening skills. *There is a difference in hearing someone speak as opposed to listening to the words they've spoken.*

* * * * *

The act of hearing is a process of transmitted sound waves to the ear and into the brain, where the words are transformed into clear information. It is a passive quality that can occur even while you sleep. Hearing someone's words, but not listening to what's being said may be just the thing that leads to misunderstandings, missed opportunities, and discontent between you and your community [customer].

> *There's a lot of difference between listening and hearing.*
> —G. K. Chesterton
> Journalist, Dramatist, Orator

Tip 88: Use Your Ears and Eyes to Listen

Listening is a physical experience. Often, our interpersonal relationships thrive or fail due to the lack of or the breakdown in communication. The manner in which we communicate can be detrimental to the message being sent and received, particularly in the interrelationship area between community policing and customer service.

* * * * *

Our body language, our tone of voice, and feelings communicate louder than the words we speak in most instances. Do you take listening seriously? Research has shown that 7% of our communication comes from words we use, 38% is determined by how we say words; the tone of voice and style; and 55% of active communication is determined by facial expressions and body language (Mehrabian, 1967).

> *Listen, or your tongue will make you deaf.*
> —Native American Proverb

Tip 89: Practice Active Listening

Without a doubt, if you seek to attain the benefits of effective communication skills, you must be willing to learn how to listen. The act of truly listening means to *absorb the intention of the words and sentences being spoken,* thereby, grasping an understanding of the facts or ideas in your brain.

* * * * *

Your ability to focus entirely on what the communicator is saying and is not saying, to understand the meaning of what is said in its intended context of the expressed desire and then to support the communicator, is the essence of active listening.

> *The word listen contains the same letters as the word silent.*
> —Alfred Brendé
> Austrian Pianist

Tip 90: Listening: Key to Learning in Community Relations — Umoja

During times when communities face sensitive issues, your ability to be active in the process of communication and relationship building are on the front lines. Engaging in community relationship sessions provides the distinct opportunity to learn and grow as communication becomes the key to creating *Umoja* and understanding cultural differences.

* * * * *

In facing cultural differences, the residents and community police leaders should conduct community through listening sessions to engage and learn about the community's perspectives and views. When Charleston, NC, experienced a sensitive racial crime that devastated the community, it was determined that a source of (*Umoja*) unity between the police department and the community was a must. Valuable learning took place through the many community relations sessions, which revealed the community's feelings of victimization as it mourned the senseless loss of nine of its community leaders. The vocal sessions were instrumental as community police and officials listened to the victimized community's views. Unity resulted in teamwork and hopes for long-term success in healing and finding resolution to this NC community's concerns.

> *The most basic of all human needs is the need to understand and be understood. The best way to understand people is to listen to them.*
> —Dr. Ralph Nichols
> ILA Listening Hall of Fame, Inductee

Tip 91: Listen Without Opinion

When you listen to someone, you should discard your views and all your preconceived ideas. *You should just hear at that moment and not allow personal thoughts to interfere with what is being said.*

* * * * *

Typically, when we are supposed to be engaged in listening, we are not. Instead, we hear what's been said as an echo of ourselves. This echo of yourself is…your opinion. If you are listening to your views and if that person agrees with your opinion, then you accept it. But, if it is not in agreement with your views, then you reject it, or you may not even hear or understand what that person had to say.

> *Most people do not listen with the intent to understand; they listen with the intent to reply.*
> —Stephen R.Covey, Author
> *Habit #6 Synergize*

Tip 92: Listen to Build Trust, Credibility, and Customer Service Excellence

Listening alone is a real supportive activity that people appreciate, especially when they are upset or otherwise concerned. While practicing your community policing, during times when your customers (community) are facing stress, your ability to listen will show respect and empathy for those you serve in the community.

* * * * *

By listening, you are sending a message that says: "*You are important to me and I respect you.*" Listening thus boosts a customer's sense of identity. Also, people who listen are trusted more than those who grab the talking stick and barge straight into chatter, as trust is the catalyst to changing minds. In Richmond, VA, community police listened and built trust with a community of people who had special needs by assisting the legislative system in passing a law called JP's Law. The law allowed people to voluntarily add a code to their driver's license to let police know that they have autism or an intellectual disability.

> *To say that a person feels listened to means a lot more than just their ideas get heard. It's a sign of respect. It makes people feel valued.*
>
> —Deborah Tannen
> American Linguistic Professor

Tip 93: Acknowledge Conflicts; Not Avoidance

Conflict can sometimes be destructive. In the end, people can develop negative feelings for each other and spend vast amounts of energy engaged in senseless turmoil. Conflict also has the tendency to deepen differences and lead people of different cultural backgrounds, ethnicities, and races to become polarized in their corners. However, *if the conflict is well-managed, it can also be constructive by acknowledging and clearing the air; releasing emotions and stress; and by providing mediation or resolution of the issue.*

* * * * *

"Response" to conflict is related to your perceptions. Objectivity of the facts is the least concern of *"Response"* to conflict. Perceptions tend to be influenced by life experiences, culture, values, and beliefs. We need to be understood, nurtured, and supported in seeking conflict resolution.

Resolutions to Conflict Begin With:

- *Controlling your emotions and your actions.*
- *Paying attention to the feelings of those involved and the verbiage you use.*
- *Being aware of and being respectful of differences. expressed both verbally and non-verbally.*

> *Conflict can and should be handled constructively; when it is, relationships benefit. Conflict avoidance is not the hallmark of a good relationship. On the contrary, it is a symptom of serious problems and poor communication.*
>
> —Harriet B. Braiker, Author
> *Who's Pulling Your Strings?*

Tip 94: Embrace the Value of Listening

Study after study has shown that listening is critical to leadership effectiveness. So, why are so few leaders good at engaging in efficient community relations?

* * * * *

The answer is simple: *There are times when leadership's involvement in community relationship discussions becomes overbearing.* In this instance, leadership attempts to take command, direct the conversations, talk too much, or worry about what they will say next in defense or rebuttal. Rather, it is crucial on the part of leadership to show evidence of caring about what members of a community have to say about the issues at hand.

> *Of all the skills of leadership, listening is the most valuable — and one of the least understood. Most leaders listen only sometimes. But, a few great ones, never stop listening. That's how they get the word before anyone else concerning unseen problems and opportunities.*
>
> —Peter Nulty
> *National Business Hall of Fame Fortune Magazine*

Tip 95: Listen and Understand Disagreements

Accepting and embracing disagreements and controversy can be complicated for some in leadership positions. Community policing agents generally have tendencies to seek harmony and cooperation with their customers most of the time. On its face this may seem impractical. Yet, without dissent and differing opinions, the world would be a very bland, boring, and a conformist place.

* * * * *

Embracing disagreement is a valuable way of learning new points of view from the customers in the community you serve. It also offers an opportunity to soften your thoughts and ideas, and thereby, reach desirable or amicable solutions. If you develop your listening skills and learn to accept dissent when engaging in disagreements, then your interpersonal relations within the community you serve may significantly improve.

> A good listener tries to understand what the other person is saying. In the end they may disagree sharply, but because they disagree, they want to know exactly what it is they are disagreeing with.
> —Kenneth A. Wells
> *A Guide to Good Leadership*

Tip 96: Practice Silence Techniques

If you learn the skill of silence, you also have improved your listening. Silence can be beneficial in active communication. But for some, going on a long automobile trip with someone who cannot stand silence can make for a very challenging ride. Some people can't stand silence and will talk just to fill the silent space.

* * * * *

Your projection, your perception, and the manner in which you conduct yourself in a community meeting can be extremely critical to the success of the meeting. When in a meeting, don't be one of the first to give a comment. Remember, as a community policing agent, you are also an authority figure and you do not want to appear to know it all. If you wait to be the third or fourth person to speak, you will have a better understanding of the "context" of the situation.

Often, when listening, we can't wait to talk. *Our goal should be instead to pause three to four seconds before responding.* Count mentally "one thousand one," "one thousand two," etc., and then speak. Counting down in this manner allows the speaking person to provide you, the listener, with more and sometimes better information.

Practicing silence allows you to pay attention to the nonverbal communication, while allowing you to really hear what is being said.

> *" I remind myself every morning:*
> *Nothing I say this day will teach me anything.*
> *So if I'm going to learn, I must do it by listening.*
>
> —Larry King
> Entertainer

Tip 97: Silence Is Good for Mental Alertness

People who are not uncomfortable with silence are more *likely to learn from the silence, and be more mentally alert and appreciated.*

* * * * *

As our internal and external worlds become louder and louder, people are beginning to seek out silence, whether through a practice of sitting quietly for 10 minutes at the beginning of the morning or heading off to a 10-day silent retreat. The benefits are favorable as noise can lead to high blood pressure, heart attacks, and raised stress levels. *Silence can release varying degrees of tension and positively impact physical health.*

Research has shown that silence plays a significant part in higher-order thinking, decision-making, problem-solving, and learning. *When your brain is allowed to be idled and disengaged from external stimuli, the ability to access your inner stream of thoughts, emotions, memories, and ideas is notable.* You can do this by breaking away from the distractions that may hold you in the shallow surfaces of your mind. Silence is one way to get there.

> *I've begun to realize that you can listen to silence and learn from it. It has a quality and a dimension all its own.*
>
> —Chaim Potok, Author
> *In the Beginning*

Tip 98: Engage in Questions and Listen to Gain Wisdom

Even if you are an expert in your field of community policing, you do not have all the answers. The one thing you can consistently strive to do is to seek to understand and find the experts. *Find the people whom you can ask the pertinent questions and provide you with the appropriate answers that will help you achieve wisdom.* Take notes and remember the beginner's mindset. Be curious, ask questions, maintain the beginner's mind, and focus on those who have preceded you.

> *Effective questioning brings insight, which fuels curiosity, which cultivates wisdom.*
>
> —Chip Bell
> Public Speaker

Tip 99: Your Reflection Is Viewed by the Way You Treat Others

How you treat others can be a reflection of you and the way you look at the world. It reflects how you feel about life, particularly, your life.

* * * * *

Someone who is never content or happy with life, or a person who thinks nothing is ever good enough, is often a person who probably treats other people poorly, as well. Their unhappiness with life and their surroundings makes them likely to be discontent with everyone they encounter. This unhappiness can be a noticeable problem. You may not think others notice, but they do. In fact, you may believe that it is everyone else who has a problem, but in reality, you are probably the problem.

You are the only one in control of your thoughts. If you encounter, say 100 people over time, and they are all out to get you, wouldn't it make more sense to the premise that possibly, it is *"just you and your attitude"*? In this instance, you are, after all, the one common denominator in every situation that involves you. If you go out into the world looking for a fight, you will find one that you have created all by yourself! If you change your thoughts and change your words, you will see that people you encounter will begin to engage with you differently. The way people act towards you is a direct reflection of how you feel about yourself and how you, in turn, make them feel.

This is relevant because your presence as a community

policing agent should make people feel special, significant, and important in the process of active communication in community discussions. When people, particularly people who are different from you, feel good about the way that you treat them when interacting with them, you are adding value to their presence and building stable relationships.

> *Great leadership isn't shaped in the absence of opposition but the presence of it. Great leaders draw us together by our universal humanity; they galvanize the will of the willing; they draw clarity from the spigot of chaos.*
>
> —Maya Angelou
> American Artist, Poet

Tip 100: Listen to Your Inner-Self vs. Your Ego

For most people, one's ego is not an issue. It's only when someone has too much ego, which they are considered egotistical, that it does become an issue. A hyper-ego is usually a significant challenge at first. It takes practice to recognize the difference between listening to your authentic inner-self (intuition) and ego-based messages. The ego must be guided by a wiser element, and that is the inner or higher self.

* * * * *

We perceive the ability to think as a natural gift that humans enjoy. Your ability to gain insight into your inner self and interpret the intuitions that you receive means that you are using your original thinking gift for its ultimate purpose. The complication lies in your ability to determine which entity to listen to — ego or inner voice. An example of listening to your inner-self is starting a business to help others, as opposed to listening to your ego and starting a business to become rich.

You will be able to distinguish the differences when you find yourself contemplating a situation that seems contradictory, and suddenly the entire situation makes sense to you. *At that moment, you will experience enlightenment as this process unfolds.*

> " *Never allow your ego to diminish your ability to listen.*
>
> —Gary Hopkins Author
> *Angel Talks*

Tip 101: Face Your Weaknesses

Now, that you are reading and reviewing the dynamics that can or have challenged you in your work in community policing as you provide customer service excellence, what improvements can you individually make to move forward professionally? Are there any areas that you would like to strengthen? Can you identify any weaknesses? If so, the best way to turn a weakness around is to face those deficiencies and look into any existing opportunities. Once again, you have to determine the areas you need to improve upon and then take action to turn your weaknesses into strengths.

* * * * *

While looking to others for encouragement is great, it is important that you not allow yourself to be trapped by looking for their approval, as well. You must face your weaknesses.

Sandra, for example, was a Captain in a southern metro police department. She found herself flailing in her ability to successfully multi-task her work and her responsibilities. Often, Sandra found herself pre-occupied or unable to focus on her work in the community.

However, in facing her weakness, she focused on a to-do list. The Captain ranked her duties by priority and placed the list in a visible area at home and on her cell phone. The daily reminders kept her on track as she successfully tackled her duties that left her feeling a sense of accomplishment. *Remembering that your weaknesses, disadvantages, or challenges can become your strengths is a valuable concept to embrace.*

> *Never let a weakness convince you that you lack strength.*
> —Unknown Author

Summary

What do the Green Bay Police Department, Abu Dhabi Police GHQ, Armstrong University Police Department, Toronto Police Service, New South Wales Police Department, New Zealand Police Department and the Sidney Australia Police Department all have in common? All of these police departments have received Customer Service Excellence (CSE) Awards. Each of these policing units has evolved into organizations of consistent and constant teamwork that took on the challenges of providing their communities with customer service that went "above and beyond" their customer's expectations.

Customer service applies to anyone in a service sector position, including police officers. Whether serving on the police force for a city, school, or a security guard for a neighborhood, some level of customer service skills is necessary for providing services. However, if high levels of trust, respect, and partnership between customers and community police are the intended goals, then, CSE must be the target goal. For example, CSE means more than acting professionally and being in proper uniform or giving directions and assistance. It's also more than pulling a stopped vehicle over to a safe place, immediately identifying oneself through name and badge, and explicitly stating the reason for the stop. It means more than the application of tactical skills and the knowledge of survival while serving and protecting. The practice of CSE means that police who work within the community, be it the general community or a college/university campus, etc., will also go above and beyond the expectations of the customers they serve.

By instituting CSE, community policing takes on a new aspect in addressing and serving the citizenry, particularly cross-cultural and multicultural communities, where behavior, identities, and languages play dominant roles in the community establishment. As an investment in the community, CSE results in stronger community ties, harmony, trust and mutual support. In return, the stronger emotional connection between the community policing department and the served community can co-exist. Their co-existence begins with insightful and purposeful leadership while acknowledging the need for courteous and respectful collaboration within the community.

Additionally, leadership command must include a constant and consistent focus on the development and regimental training of soft skills enlightenment, which goes beyond the conventional tactical and criminal justice training. Soft skills training must include levels of mastery for those community officers who have daily contact with the community they serve. The personal mastery of self-awareness, self-development, attitude positioning, setting goals, customer service, communication, and active listening are critical to the community policing agent's ability to know and understand the culture and the needs of the customers they serve.

The bottom line is simple. If CSE is the aspirational goal of uniting a community or if CSE is already being implemented, then the intended outcome for your organization should be the formal education of leadership and enhanced focus. These efforts embrace highly evolved levels of communication and collaboration between "community policing agents who serve and their delivery of customer service excellence."

Afterword

"A person or group of people can suffer real damage, real distortion if the people or society around them mirror back to them a confining or demeaning or contemptible picture of themselves."

— Melissa Harris-Perry Author, Educator, Journalist

The Historical Patterns of Denial, Rejection, and Trauma

On this soil, trauma has taken an earlier path: one that spread from the bodies of European colonists to the bodies of Native people by genocide, and then through many generations of their descendants. It was a time in which equality and justice were evasive. An estimated 18 million people were custodians of this land when colonized Europeans arrived. Native people and their ancestors had lived for an estimated 14,000 years.

Today, this American soil contains over 204 million White Americans, over 46 million Black Americans, just over five million Native Americans with the remaining 116 million people extending from other lands and countries throughout the world. The unique arc of trauma in the Native American body is a story that is only beginning to be told as society maintains its long-standing denial of acceptance of Native American generational culture, rights, voice, and community relationship building. This persistent and corrosive denial of the acceptance of others has proven to be universal. It has historically and chronically damaged the mindsets of people who claim power while they face the recent traumas of people as a result of the impact of globalization. The inundation of streams of peoples searching for freedoms, financial security, and physical safety is the new phenomenon as international uprisings, genocides, and the quest for power and oppressive actions grow exponentially.

As a mental health trauma specialist, I continue to hold onto the hope that Native American people receive recognition as the foundational fabric of this land. I also continue to hope that justice leadership will prevail as their voices and the voices of the dejected and rejected will be heard at the table, as well. It is my hope that people with power will examine their interpersonal and relationship skills while interacting with the diverse communities they serve. I offer my respect and acknowledge Native American people as the stewards of this soil long before African and European descendants first came to this land and before denial and acceptance became the norm of today.

Lastly, this book uniquely lays down the ground work for several community principles, *Umoja, Ujima and Kuumba*, as well as the personal principles of *Nia* and *Kujichagulia,* as community policing agents and diverse communities seek to build successful interpersonal relationships.

—Resmaa Menakem, LCSW
CEO Justice Leadership Solutions *Life Leadership & Legacy: 101 Tips for Emerging Justice Leaders*

Endnotes

1. Pronunciation of Kujichagulia: Swahili terminology. https://www.youtube.com/watch?v=Fd_zRk4NCqQ

2. Nia: Swahili terminology

3. Kuumba: Swahili terminology

4. Pronunciation of Umoja: Swahili terminology https://www.youtube.com/watch?v=Aq86jwzJGDI

5. Pronunciation of Ujima: Swahili terminology https://www.youtube.com/watch?v=CNONqjbt8ys

NOTES

As you view these 101 TIPS, you will have an opportunity to embrace your thoughts as to how you may be able to apply them in your professional and personal life as well. Take a moment to write how these tips relate to you and how you will put these tips into action as you communicate and establish the vast number of interpersonal relationships that you encounter during your journey of providing customer service excellence.

Chapter 1: Mastery of Self-Awareness

Tip 1: Open Your Mind

Tip 2: Be Consistent: Take the Long Road in Your Work

Tip 3: Kujichagulia: Take Responsibility

Tip 4: Nia: Embrace the Art of Giving

Tip 5: Be Authentic

Tip 6: Transform Your Image

Tip 7: Conquer Your Fear of Failure

Tip 8: Practice Self-Confidence & Belief in Yourself

Tip 9: Take Time for Reflection

Tip 10: Review Your Perspectives and Judgment

Tip 11: Become an Expert—
Application and Practice Mean Everything

Tip 12: Understand Your Implicit Biases

Chapter 2: Mastery of Self Development

Tip 13: Embrace Your Discomfort
to Find New Opportunities

Tip 14: Don't Buy Into Shortcuts and Temporary Solutions

Tip 15: Nia: Purposefully Manifest Your Dreams

Tip 16: Kuumba: Use Creativity in the Law of Attraction

Tip 17: Appreciate Your Contributions

Tip 18: Be Flexible and Adaptable to Differences

Tip 19: Improve Your Efficiency

Tip 20: Know What You Don't Know and Seek Input

Tip 21: You Don't Have to Settle

Tip 22: Umoja: Be a Good Leader — A Good Servant

Tip 23: Seek Out, Enroll, and Welcome Training

Tip 24: Don't Run from Change

Tip 25: Balance the Concepts of "Ordinary and Comfortable" in Your Life

Tip 26: Don't Rest on Success

Tip 27: Take Initiative—Apply What You Learn

Tip 28: Keep a Journal – It's Healthy

Tip 29: Engage Priorities – Be Proactive

Tip 30: Offer Praise and Recognition

Tip 31: Don't Be Complacent: Harmful to a Beginner's Mind

Tip 32: Practice Empathy With Your Job Performance

Chapter 3: Mastery of Attitude Possession
Tip 33: Be Happy: It's All About Attitude

Tip 34: Kujichagulia and an Unstoppable Attitude

Tip 35: By All Means Have Courage

Tips 36: Embrace Your Passion

Tip 37: Practice Patience and Perseverance

Tip 38: Define Your Core Values

Tip 39: Grasp Humility and Be Thankful

Tip 40: Practice Rewarding Yourself

Tip 41: Celebrate Something Every Day

Tip 42: Develop Realistic Expectations

Tip 43: Practice Personal Tolerance

Tip 44: Use Your Work Positively

Tip 45: Culture Shock? Be Excited and Not Stagnant

Tip 46: Eliminate the Toxic Poisoning

Tip 47: Surround Yourself with Like Minds

Tip 48: Be Positive and Be Passionate…It's Healthy

Tip 49: Focus On Solutions

Tip 50: Select Strengths vs. Flaws

Tip 51: Treat Individuals As a Person and Not a Stereotype

Tip 52: View Your Job As a Positive Force

Tip 53: Your Contagious Attitude

Tip 54: Ujima: Collectivity & Global Citizenry

Tip 55: Examine Your Interactive Reflections

Tip 56: Maintain Dignity in Cultural Differences

Tip 57: Recognize and Respond

Chapter 4: Mastery of Setting Goals

Tip 58: Set Clear Goals

Tip 59: Are Your Goals Reachable, Timely?

Tip 60: Take Advantage of Goal-Oriented Training

Tip 61: Align Your Goals With One Another

Tip 62: Visualize Yourself in Your Goals

Tip 63: Give Up Your Morals for Your Goals?

Tip 64: Share Your Success

Chapter 5: Mastery of Community and Customer Service Excellence Skills

Tip 65: Understand Community Policing

Tip 66: Know the Community Leadership

Tip 67: Attract Your Community with Customer Service Excellence

Tip 68: Be Involved in Your Community

Tip 69: Make Opportunities for Interaction

Tip 70: Develop a "We" — "Umoja" Mentality

Tip 71: Create Value by Focusing on Customer Service Excellence

Tip 72: Be Efficient in Giving Excellent Service

Tip 73: Cultural Differences in Delivering Customer Service Excellence

Tip 74: Identifying Quality Customer Service Excellence

Tip 75: Kujichagulia: Be Self-Determined and Open to New Ideas

Tip 76: Trust in Community Policing Creates Customer Service Excellence

Tip 77: Neighborhood Partnering

Tip 78: The Right Support Team and Residency Training

Tip 79: Review International Policing Collaborations

Tip 80: Umoja: School Collaborations

Tip 81: Choose Triumph vs. Trying

Tip 82: Embrace Your Social Engagement

Tip 83: Practice Self-Care

Tip 84: Create Opportunities for Openness in Customer Service

Tip 85: Identify Barriers to Enabling Openness in Customer Service Excellence

Chapter 6: Mastery of Communication and Effective Listening

Tip 86: Know Your High and Low Context in Communication

Tip 87: Know the Differences Between Listening and Hearing

Tip 88: Use Your Ears and Eyes to Listen

Tip 89: Practice Active Listening

Tip 90: Listening: The Key to Learning in Community Relations — Umoja

Tip 91: Listen Without Opinion

Tip 92: Listen to Build Trust, Credibility, and Customer Service Excellence

Tip 93: Acknowledge Conflicts; Not Avoidance

Tip 94: Embrace The Value of Listening

Tip 95: Listen and Understand Disagreements

Tip 96: Practice Silence Techniques

Tip 97: Silence Is Good for Mental Alertness

Tip 98: Engage in Questions and Listen to Gain Wisdom

Tip 99: Your Reflection Is Viewed by the Way You Treat Others

Tip 100: Listen to Your Inner-Self vs. Your Ego

Tip 101: Face Your Weaknesses

Acknowledgments

I always wanted to be somebody. If I made it, it is half because I was game enough to take a lot of punishment along the way and half because there were a lot of people who cared enough to help me.
—Althea Gibson
Athlete

This book, *Customer Service Excellence for Police: 101 Tips on Policing in Cross-Cultural Communities*, is devoted to the concepts of communal togetherness via servant leadership, justice leadership, and responsibility. Just as the 17th century's Age of Enlightenment ushered in reasoning, mental capacity, and logical formation, its purpose intended to provide knowledge and understanding based on evidence and proof. Today, we recognize that enlightenment is the source of awareness, particularly self-awareness. Self-awareness is important in our ability to recognize our uniqueness as separate individuals. This is key to understanding, developing, and improving our interpersonal relationships with others whose backgrounds may appear to be different from ours. *Customer Service Excellence for Police: 101 Tips on Policing in Cross-Cultural Communities* offers a harmonious learning environment as it is rooted in the historical context and meaningfulness of knowledge and understanding. It identifies the processes and practical skills that you will need to become an emerging justice leader by placing a staunch emphasis on compassion, communication, and self-reflection in cross-cultural communities.

I would not have envisioned this book and laced these written words together without the guidance and assistance from those who walked before me and next to me in both my professional and personal lives. Their shared wisdom and teachings provided supportive environments and models for my emulation and growth. I give heartful thanks to my dearest family members, friends, and professional acquaintances who supported my goals and desires (knowingly and unknowingly) to create this book of communal relationship building through awareness and personal skill development. I want to offer special thanks to Coaching Firm International and its highly efficient team for their role in my mastery of coaching development and growth. And to my mother, father, and brother, I continue to feel your encompassing presence as I move through, share and reflect upon the precious meanings of life, engagement, and fulfillment.

Adissa Justice Leadership Coaching

"Because Serving Others Is What You Do Best"

What is Coaching?

Coaching is a form of development in which a person called a coach supports a learner or client in achieving a specific personal or professional goal by providing training, advice, and guidance. The learner is called a coachee.

Why do you need Justice Leadership Coaching?

Coaching helps you to grow, focus, and resolve the things that contribute to your feelings of being stuck. Coaching helps you to examine your perceptions, attitudes, and the internal drives that may conflict with your growth and progress as you exhibit your awareness of justice leadership, compassion, and fairness in the community you serve as a committed servant leader.

Why do you need Adissa Justice Leadership Coaching?

AJLC provides you with the soft skill techniques to help you grow, focus, and resolve those elements that contribute to your feelings of being stuck in your work and your self-actualization. We assist you in examining your perceptions, attitude, and internal drives that may conflict with or stifle your forward progression in the work or services you provide in the community.

Here's What Coaching Can Do For You

AJLC can:

- ⇾ **Bolster Your Creativity**
- ⇾ **Help You Raise Your Self-Awareness Levels**
- ⇾ **Boost Productivity and Effectiveness**
- ⇾ **Develop Your Communication Skills**
- ⇾ **Bring Work-life Balance Into Existence**
- ⇾ **Help You Thrive in Your Work**
- ⇾ **Build/Restore Self-Confidence**
- ⇾ **Provide Tools For LeadershipDevelopment**
- ⇾ **Help You Resolve Conflicts**

If any of these areas of assistance represent the tools, you need to move forward in your community service and relationship building; then your next step is to partner with Dr. Coleman-Mason at AJLC. We have the expertise to meet your needs. Our customer service training/coaching program offers opportunities to help you establish the service strategies for the customers you serve.

Justice Customer Service Excellence

Customer Service Excellence is more than merely satisfying your community customers. It means to provide exceptional service that goes beyond the customer's expectations. To the customer, it's the feeling of being pleasantly surprised. We provide you with sound practical strategies to assist you in the Mastery of Community and Customer Service Skills that help you to engage with your community; make opportunities for interaction; understand the cultural differences while delivering excellent service; promote trust among community members; counter the barriers to customer service excellence; and develop self-care methods.

Training Service Offerings

At AJLC, we offer a unique self-awareness tool. The online FryePush.com tool offers you an opportunity to develop your self-awareness as it concerns your wellness and leadership as you engage with multi-cultural communities and build those important relationships. The customized in-person and web-based leadership workshops provide navigation in the dynamics of race, organizational inclusion and matters of de-escalation and conflict resolution. Group coaching and passionate speaking engagements for teams can be accessed and made available by request. AJLC's unique concept intends to motivate you into bringing forth specific leadership qualities, which may have been thwarted in the past. The goal is to develop and blend these sound strategies, skills, and techniques with your commitment and values to make a strong difference. Amanda and AJLC are here to partner with you and to coach you toward your next level of productivity in providing customer service excellence and justice leadership.

"Because Serving Others Is What You Do Best"

Contact the Doctor at:
Adissa Justice Leadership Coaching
www.adissajusticeleadership.com
amanda@adissajusticeleadership.com
414-828-0242

About the Authors

Dr. Amanda Coleman-Mason

Dr. Amanda Coleman-Mason is a Professor of Human Services and Community Social Work at the University of North Texas, Dallas; a national speaker; an international coach and consultant to the UAE Police Department; and the creative and visionary mind behind the development and implementation of Adissa Justice Leadership Coaching (AJLC). As an open-minded visionary and a lifelong learner, she prides herself on new ideas and innovative concepts related to the delivery system of human services and community needs. Those closest to her believe that she maintains this mindset, due to her passions and her life views. The cornerstone of her life views is embedded in a well-known quote by A. J. McLean:

Be very, very patient and very open-minded and listen to what people have to say.

Amanda sees her open-mindedness as a driving instrument in developing and providing the specific training and coaching of soft-skills techniques for community policing. Through AJLC, she provides these endeavors, both locally and internationally while embracing her drive and passion for engagement in activities as a servant leader, as well.

The primary function of AJLC is to provide effective soft-skill training courses & coaching sessions with an emphasis on Customer Service Excellence in community policing in cross-cultural communities. It is critical to note that the strategies and techniques implemented in AJLC's soft skills training are not intended to replace or alter criminal justice, or tactical skills. Rather, AJLC's intentions is to assist teams, organizations, and community policing agents in establishing customer service excellence and effective behavioral strategies while building community relationships among cross-cultural communities.

Dr. Coleman-Mason's effective AJLC coaching curriculum leads to competencies that enhance community policing agent's skills by offering tips on skill building through Mastery Level concepts that include: a) Mastery of Self-Awareness; b) Mastery of Self-Development; c) Mastery of Attitude Possession; d) Mastery of Goal Setting; e) Mastery of Community & Customer Service; f) and Mastery of Communication & Effective Listening.

Dr. Coleman-Mason resides in North Texas where she surrounds herself with family members and friends. In her leisure time, she prides herself on growing her organic garden and taking part in one of her favorite pastimes; riding Pearl, her Harley Davidson motorcycle.

"Because Serving Others Is What You Do Best"

Dr. Amanda Coleman-Mason
Adissa Justice Leadership Coaching
www.adissajusticeleadership.com
amanda@adissajusticeleadership.com
414-828-0242

June Davidson, PhD

Dr. June Davidson is the co-author with Dr. Coleman-Mason on the writing of Customer Service Excellence for Police: 101 Tips on Policing in Cross-Cultural Communities. June Davidson is President of the American Seminar Leaders Association, (ASLA) and President of Coaching Firm International (CFI). As a master trainer, she writes curriculum and trains others to create their seminar curriculum in their identified niche. At CFI, trainees and coaches define their well-defined niche, similar to the type of specialization often found in large law firms. Her teaching style is based on experiential and accelerated learning. Action Coaches certified by CFI receive thorough training that equips each person with unique tools, such as ATAP (Access the Truth Accelerator your Process) ™, and methods for rapid brain pattern interrupts. Over the years she has made an impact on countless lives. As an activist, June founded Women Against Child Trafficking, a U. S. non-profit organization. As a platform speaker at major events, she won numerous awards. Her accolades include the recipient of the 2013 Social Entrepreneur of the Year Award for enlightening and empowering women of all ages; and the 2011 coveted Women of Excellence award by NAFE. Dr. Davidson is a visionary whose intention is to help others succeed, never once not thinking about "What can I do for you?"

Contact Dr. June Davidson at:
American Seminar Leaders Association (ASLA): asla.com
Coaching Firm International CFI
http://www.coaching firminternational.com
Email: June@asla.com
Phone: 626-791-1211

www.ingramcontent.com/pod-product-compliance
Lightning Source LLC
Chambersburg PA
CBHW070605010526
44118CB00012B/1450